Against the World

The Odyssey
of Athanasius

Against the World

The Odyssey
of Athanasius

by

Henry W. Coray

INHERITANCE PUBLICATIONS
NEERLANDIA, ALBERTA, CANADA
PELLA, IOWA, U.S.A.

Canadian Cataloguing in Publication Data

Coray, Henry W.
 Against the world

 ISBN 0-921100-35-3

 1. Athanasius, Saint, Patriarch of Alexandria,
d. 373. I. Title
BR1720.a7c67 1992   270.2'092   c92-091436-5

Library of Congress Cataloging-in-Publication Data

Coray, Henry W.
 Against the world : the odyssey of Athanasius / Henry W. Coray.
  p.   cm.
 ISBN 0-921100-35-3
 1. Athanasius, Saint, Patriarch of Alexandria, d. 373.
2. Christian saints—Egypt—Alexandria—Biography. 3. Alexandria
(Egypt)
—Biography. I. Title.
BR1720.A7C67 1992
270.2'092—dc20
[B]   92-36828
                                                                           CIP

3rd Printing 2006

Cover Picture by Yvonne Harink

Published simultaneously in U.S.A. by Inheritance Publications
Box 366, Pella, Iowa 50219

Available in Australia from Inheritance Publications
Box 1122, Kelmscott, W.A. 6111 Tel. & Fax (089) 390 4940

Printed in Canada

**To Jim Packer
Whose life and writings have been
a real inspiration to me.**

FOREWORD

We have seldom an opportunity of observing, either in active or speculative life, what effect may be produced, or what obstacles may be surmounted by the force of a single mind, when it is inflexibly applied to the pursuit of a single object. The immortal name of Athanasius will never be separated from the catholic doctrine of the Trinity, to whose defense he consecrated every moment and every faculty of his being.

Edward Gibbon

This tribute, coming from the pen of an historian who entertained very little sympathy for the Christian faith, was in fact the very paragraph that sparked my desire to set forth the story of Athanasius.

Against the World is a fictionalized profile of the subject. Much of the material is culled from the writings of reliable church historians. Various segments, however, are the products of human imagination. For example, there are, in the record, few details given us of the business proceedings and vigorous debates that took place in the momentous Council of Nicea. I, nevertheless, have tried to set forth honestly the spirit and temper of that and other councils as well as the character and personality of the man who occupies the centerpiece, certainly one of the most redoubtable nobleman in the pantheon of Christian statesmen.

It is with this in mind that I hope that the odyssey of the Father of Orthodoxy might be delineated in a way that will challenge all readers to a stronger commitment to the God-Man for whom Athanasius sacrificed and suffered.

Henry W. Coray

Chapter 1

In 331 B.C., Alexander the Great founded the city named in his honor. At the time, the Ptolemies were in control of Egypt. Two centuries later, Cleopatra, the last ruler of the Ptolemy dynasty, passed away. The Roman emperor Octavius promptly took over Egypt with its rich lands and thriving communities, including Alexandria, often referred to as the Golden City.

Alexander had directed his architect, Dinocrates, to design a center that would endure as a lasting memorial to him. The result: Alexandria was fashioned into a perfect rectangle five miles long and a mile wide. Two broad boulevards lined with snowy colonnades intersected at right angles. The longer one stretched from the Hippodrome on the east to the Necropolis on the west. The shorter of the two connected the southern Gate of the Sun to the northern Gate of the Moon. Granite quays studded the shoreline, which overlooked flotillas of grain ships lolling on the surface of the Mediterranean.

Seven miles out at sea on the island of Phares, a wall of chalk cliffs climbed four hundred feet into the air. It was here that the Septuagint, the Greek version of the Hebrew Scriptures, was completed by seventy scholars. At one end of the seven wonders of the ancient world, a cone of pure marble had been built to guide mariners through the treacherous limestone shoals.

If Alexandria received praise for its physical beauty, conversely, it had earned the reputation of being a caldron of licentiousness. Internal corruption contaminated much of its social life. Homosexuality and incest flourished unashamed. Almost with pride, Strabo reported that he had made overtures to a boy who sold flowers and berries on the street. Emperor Hadrian, no paragon on virtue himself, professed shock at the sights and sounds he took in when he first entered the port.

Like Gaul, Alexandria was divided into three parts: the Egyptian, the Greek, and the Jewish quarters. Seafaring folk occupied the Egyptian sector. Here stood the Serapeium, the temple of Serapis, god of the underworld. The shrine represented a blend of the deities Osiris and Apis with the adoration of the Greek gods

Zeus and Pluto. Also to be seen in this district was the less imposing of two internationally famous libraries: Alexandrines called the Daughter.

The Greek section, wedged between the Egyptian and the Jewish areas, was the largest of the three districts. Here sprawled the Museion (Museum), declared to be the greatest of intellectual achievements of the age. It fostered the Mother, the more ornate of the two libraries. Over 500,000 books lined its shelves. The Museion also included a number of lecture halls, laboratories, observatories, a dining hall, a park, and even a zoo.

Other features in the Hellenistic section were the Soma, a mausoleum containing the body of Alexander the Great, the Dicasterium, the Senate chamber, the Exchange (or Emporium), a gymnasium, a stadium, a theater, a race course.

The Jewish quarter incorporated the northeastern slice of the city. Jews enjoyed equal rights with other citizens and were governed by their own provincial ruler. They had their laws, their Sanhedrin, their synagogue. Unfortunately, between them and the Hellenistic Alexandrines severe internecine tensions sometimes mounted. Then it was that tempers flared, riots erupted, and the streets of this part of the Golden City flowed with crimson.

Philosophically, the ideas of Plato permeated the thinking of Alexandria's intelligentsia. At Athens, the philosopher had projected the notion that the present world is a copy of the ideal world. In Egypt, this seed took the form of "the white mystic rose of Neoplatonism." The Neoplatonist school came to full fruition under the tutelage of a scholar, one Plotinus. Plotinus mixed portions of Scripture with the formulations of Plato, stirred in a sprinkling of Hindu doctrine, and tried to relate feeble humanity in a succession of semigods, demons, animals, plants, stones, and eventually the human soul. We are all parts of God, he said. People were invited to experiment with the Mystic Vision, which, when seen, would prove to the receiver that the vision of God and the vision of self were the same — this simply because each individual is in fact God!

One cannot but wonder how it was that Athanasius, destined to become the Father of Orthodoxy, coming so close to this odd milieu, escaped being drawn into the mix of pantheistic brew.

Several factors contributed to his deliverance.

The most important was the genuinely pious climate of the home, the creation of loving parents who reared their one child in the nurture and discipline of the Lord. The boy's plastic mind was regularly subjected to lessons from the Bible, together with the earnest prayers of his father. Quickly he formed the habit of writing out and memorizing long passages from the Scriptures.

Again, he was fortunate enough to come under the tutelage of Alexander, the wise and godly archbishop of Alexandria. The aging prelate, aware that his years of service were numbered, began searching the horizon with a view to selecting a successor to his office. Alexander enjoyed a position of high authority throughout Egypt. Carefully he studied the characters, personalities, and gifts of devout young men under his rule. After prolonged consideration, he became convinced that Athanasius, with his brilliant mind, would be one who should stand on his shoulders.

Alexander enrolled his ward in a catechetical school. He checked Athanasius's progress regularly. Also, he spent as much time as possible in private with him, instructing, counseling, questioning, encouraging. Secretly he rejoiced to see the way Athanasius absorbed every scrap of knowledge as a thirsty traveler takes great drafts of cold water. The archbishop confidently looked forward to the day when the student would become a polished shaft in the quiver of God — his mouth, like the mouth of Isaiah, a sharp sword, qualified to do battle for Jehovah boldly and courageously.

Athanasius implemented his formal education by investing long hours in the great library, the Mother. He loved few pursuits as much as immersing himself in the Greek and Roman classics. Then it was that for him time became nonexistent as he pored over the Categories of Aristotle, the subtle propositions of Plato, the orations of Cicero and Demosthenes, the poetry of Homer and Horace. He all but hallucinated while digesting the treatises of the church fathers: Ignatius of Antioch, the fiery Tertullian, gentle Origen, and Clement of Rome. He wept over the accounts of the martyrdoms of Polycarp, Justin Martyr, Origen, and many other heroic believers executed by order of emperors Decius and Diocletian.

The day arrived when Alexander decided that Athanasius, approaching twenty, was ready to assume his first assignment. He said, "Son, I need someone to help me with my duties. Are you prepared to go to work for me?"

Athanasius had to restrain himself from leaping for joy. "If you think I am, Sir," he said.

"I think you are. We must ask your parents if they will permit you to move into my home."

"Oh, I am sure they will, Sir. I am sure they will."

And so it was arranged.

Chapter 2

In the Roman Empire of the fourth century A.D., theology had become an enormously popular theme for discussion. Marketplaces, barber shops, hotels, parks, restaurants, and farms functioned as forums for debates; some controlled, others heated. The physician, the lawyer, the teacher, the butcher, the baker, the candlestick maker, the student, the housewife, the street-cleaner, the beggar on the corner — all discussed religion as though they were theologians of vast perceptiveness. Frequently, disputes went on far into the night.

Particularly in Alexandria, Egypt, prominent in the Roman world, it was not uncommon for fistfights to break out. The participants would then creep into bed, nursing bruised limbs, battered heads, injured jaws or noses, or missing teeth. The distinguished colors of that metropolis were black and blue.

A priest, Arius, stood out as the storm center of controversy. He served a church known as the Baukalis. Alexandrians boasted that the edifice was built over the tomb of John Mark. Mark, people said, has first brought the Christian faith to their fair city.

Arius had received his philosophical and theological training in Antioch, Syria. There, two outstanding scholars, Paulus and Lucian, had been instrumental in shaping his thinking.

Paulus, a bishop, was later deposed by order of a council of fellow bishops. There were two reasons for the action: his godless life-style and his adherence to strange, unscriptural teaching. He was accused of espousing a curious crossbreed of Platonism and Judaistic legalism, mixed with a dash of Biblical material palatable to him. Also, the Syrians knew him to be a clever sophist: he had mastered the art of double-talk.

Lucian, unlike his colleague, was a man of high moral character. But he did, with Paulus, reject the doctrine that Jesus was God incarnate. It was Lucian who coined the catch phrase, "There was a time when Jesus was not," words eventually picked up and popularized by Arius.

In personal appearance, Arius was tall, slender, and erect as obelisk. The asceticism of his manner of life showed in the lines of his face, notable for its deadly pallor. He allowed his tangled hair to fall shoulder length. He wore a mask of perpetual melancholy and dressed simply, arraying himself in a long black cloak with short sleeves, with a red scarf around his throat.

Women adored him.

Boldly he orchestrated his tenets. His syllogism was disarmingly simple: Jesus is a true Son of God. And since a father must exist before a son, temporally, it follows that the Divine Father must have existed prior to the Divine Son. Hence there was a time frame when Jesus was not. Conclusion: Jesus must be reckoned to be a created being, made of nothing. Any other definition, Arius insisted, inevitably confounds the persons of the Godhead and thus leads to serious error.

To his enthralled congregation he was nothing if not convincing.

"My system is the one safeguard against paganism," he declared from the pulpit. "In a city of learning like Alexandria, is it not the magnet destined to draw Greek and Jewish thinkers into the bosom of the church? Has it not the merit of solving the deepest mysteries of the faith? Does it not appeal to intellectuals by summoning them to the tribunal of the mind in their quest for final truth?"

Arius had begun his message in a quiet, conversational tone. But now, whipping himself into an emotional frenzy, he exchanged the normal sweetness of his voice for a harsh screaming. His eyes bulged. He pounded the pulpit. His veins throbbed and swelled. His body quivered like a frame afflicted with palsy.

"Does not my theology correct that foolish, irrational proposition that one God lives in three centers of personality?" he thundered. "Tell me, what relation has that abstract mathematical monstrosity to the basic problems facing our society, now in great ferment? No relation whatever. The truth is, it raises more questions than it purports to answer and does irreparable damage to the mind. Those who loudly proclaim the trinitarian error are sowing the wind, and I promise you they will reap the whirlwind. Mark my words."

Not content with expressing his precepts from the pulpit, he wrote a book, *Thalia* (*Happy Thoughts*), in the idiom and meter of heathen poetry. He spiced the writing with tasteless vulgarities.

The introduction is a commentary on the man's estimation of himself:

According to the faith of God's elect, who know God, sound in their creed, gifted with the Holy Spirit of God, I have received those things from partakers of wisdom, accomplished, taught of God and altogether wise. I have pursued my course with like opinions — I, the famous among men, the much-suffering for God's glory, and taught of God, I have gained wisdom and strength.

Not only locally, but also nationally, the Arian movement was beginning to take deep root. The powerful bishop of Nicodemia, Eusebius, later to become Archbishop of Constantinople, cast his lot with Arius. According to the testimony of the Goths, almost the entire Gothic nation accepted Arianism. Alaric, king of the Visigoths, and Genseric, ruler of the Vandals, embraced the doctrines and shepherded their subjects into the expanding Arian fold.

Meanwhile, Christians in Egypt waited to see if Alexander would institute disciplinary action against the cultist. They waited in vain. Alexander, although strenuously opposed to the position of Arius, did nothing.

It is ironic that the first person to come forward and brand Arius as a heretic had at one time been a professing disciple. He was Colluthus, an Alexandrian archpriest. (The office of the archpriest was a cut above the office of the priest; hence, Colluthus was superior to Arius in authority.)

There was much speculation in Egypt as to why Colluthus turned against his fellow officer. Some thought that he grew disillusioned with the rationalism of the system. Others felt that as he watched the star of Arius ascend higher and higher in the galaxy of popularity, he was stung with jealousy. Jealousy, therefore, was the lever that moved the archpriest from the camp of Arius to the more orthodox ground defended by Alexander.

Colluthus published a tract charging Arius with subverting the gospel of Christ. As evidence, he indicated that Arius was proclaiming the same heresy heralded by Paulus of Antioch. Since the Syrian church had deposed Paulus, Colluthus said, and since Arius shared the same untruths held by Paulus, Arius consequently stood condemned as a heretic.

The tract stunned Alexandrian society. It also smoked Alexander out of his shelter of silence. Now he had no choice but to reprimand the maverick priest. He sent word to Arius to meet him in private. Arius refused to confer.

Alexander then challenged Arius to a public debate. Again, Arius said no. Later, however, he entertained second thoughts. He decided that a public confrontation would provide an opportunity for him to amplify his convictions. He agreed to accept the challenge.

They came together in one of the larger lecture halls in the renowned Museion. The hall was a spacious chamber patterned in the form of an amphitheater and lined with stone benches that faced the stage.

That evening the room was filled to capacity. The citizens of the city could hardly wait to take in the debate.

Alexander opened the skirmish by reading a statement condemning the Christology of Arius. He quoted passages from printed sermons and from *Thalia* and called on the priest of Baukalis to renounce his formulations that denied the essential deity of Jesus Christ.

Arius was cunning enough to realize that assuming the offensive always gave the debater a certain psychological advantage over his opponent. He promptly counterattacked. The accused took on the role of the accuser. Arius charged his accuser with defining and defending erroneous statements concerning the person of Jesus.

Alexander was at the time approaching his seventy-fifth birthday. Conscious of his waning strength, he did not attempt to stand but seated himself on a wooden chair. He spoke slowly and with some difficulty. His eyes, however, were still as bright as beads. His features radiated a luminous glow, silent tribute to his walk with God over many decades. Neither had his mind lost any of its former acumen.

Arius remained standing during the debate.

Alexander refused to allow his adversary to take the offensive. He ignored the countercharges. In order to draw out the radical character of the teachings of Arius, he plied him with pointed questions.

"You believe, do you not, that there was a time when Jesus did not exist?" he asked.

Without the slightest hesitation, Arius replied, "I believe there was a time when Jesus did not exist."

"And do you believe that there is no true identity between the Father and the Son?" Alexander asked.

"I believe there is no true identity between the Father and the Son," Arius said firmly.

"Do you believe that there is a mere resemblance of nature in the two persons of the Godhead, Father and Son?"

Arius squirmed. Finally he said, "That, Sir, is a false question. I will not say there is a 'mere resemblance.' " I prefer to say that there is true resemblance between Father and Son."

"Do you deny that the Father and the Son coexisted from all eternity?"

Arius's eyes flashed. He replied in a rasping voice, "I have already told you that is my creed. I deny the eternal coexistence of the Father and the Son."

"And do you believe that the Son cannot know the Father and the Father's will perfectly?"

"I do so believe."

At this, a gasp went up from the audience.

Arius, aware of the shock caused by his confession, stared defiantly at the sea of faces before him.

"And do you believe," Alexander continued, "that not only does the Son *not* know the Father perfectly, but that in fact he *cannot* know the Father perfectly?"

"That I believe," Arius said.

"Then I must ask you another pivotal question," Alexander said. "You must accept the proposition that Jesus Christ, since according to you He is less than God, must, therefore, be less than a Savior. Am I right?"

Arius bit his lip. Shaking his head, he retorted, "You are putting words in my mouth. I do believe, as the Bible declares, that Jesus Christ is the Savior of the world."

"But you must believe, not that Jesus Christ is a complete and all-sufficient Savior who finished his redemptive work when He died on the cross for sinners and rose again for our salvation, but that he merely helps to save. Is that right?"

"I do believe that man must contribute to his salvation."

On that note the debate ended.

All through the session, absorbing every word with the utmost interest, there hovered in one of the wings of the stage a young man. He was so fascinated with the battle of words that when the conflict was over, he was grieved in spirit.

The young man was Athanasius.

Chapter 3

But for his confidence in the God of providence and the providence of God, Athanasius would have resented the construction of his body. He never grew taller than five feet and two inches. His enemies often sneered at him, calling him a dwarf. Emperor Julian was to label him "hardly a man, only a mannequin." Although diminutive of stature, he was blessed with a sturdy constitution. He would outlive twelve Roman emperors.

He had an unusually high forehead, a parrot like nose, deep-set, penetrating eyes. His complexion was swarthy, his hair copper colored and quite unruly. He sat and walked with a slight stoop, the result of bending over innumerable books and parchments. Except when in controversy — which was often — his expression was serene, composed.

Athanasius began his internship as personal secretary to Archbishop Alexander. He handled his master's correspondence, carried messages here and there as the situation dictated, took down sermon notes when Alexander was preparing his sermons, and generally made himself useful in the episcopal palace. He was blissfully happy, always maintaining a cheerful spirit.

He was delighted when the archbishop discussed with him certain problems that surfaced in connection with the distribution of funds to the needy members of local churches. Alexander once remarked to a friend, "I am impressed with the young man's piety and justice, candor, courtesy and kindness, and charity to the poor."

A year after Athanasius moved into the palace in A.D.320, Alexander ordained him to the office of deacon. This involved him not only in the agency of attending to the needs of unfortunate sufferers but also in activities as associate in the pulpit. On Sundays, he frequently read the Scriptures and led in prayer. He also taught catechetical classes during the week.

While functioning as a deacon, Athanasius began his career as a writer. He first produced a book, *Treatise against the Gentiles*. In a sense, the title was somewhat misleading, the contents provided a positive exposition of monotheism rather than a refutation of heathenism.

His second literary effort, *On the Incarnation*, was a masterful piece of writing and a vast improvement on his initial work. It focused on the redemptive mission of Jesus Christ. Some of his contemporaries hailed the book as the first attempt in history to present Christian truth in a philosophic-theological framework.

It was a lengthy dissertation. Actually, it consisted of fifty-six chapters. The literary style, although rambling, is marked by undertones of great moral earnestness. Moreover, it is laced with an abundance of Biblical text: 169 in all. The author dwells on such basic subjects as Jesus's virgin birth, the providence of God, the full deity of Christ (His major development), the vicarious atonement, and the resurrection of the Son.

His most stirring passage comes toward the end of the book. There he describes the triumphant advance of the kingdom of God — this in spite of the opposition of idolaters and the rising tide of Arianism:

> *Behold how the Savior's doctrine is everywhere increasing, while all idolatry and everything opposed to the faith of Christ is daily dwindling and losing power and falling. And thus beholding, worship the Savior, who is "above all," and mighty, even God the Word; and condemn those who are being worsted and done away by him. For as, when the sun is come, darkness no longer prevails, but if any is still left anywhere it is driven away; so now the divine appearing of the Word of God is come, the darkness of the idols prevails no more, and all parts of the world are illuminated by His teaching.*

The release of the two studies projected the writer into the spotlight. No longer would people, discussing scholars and pseudoscholars, ask, "Athan — who?"

Chapter 4

The outcome of the debate between Alexander and Arius had placed the archbishop in an embarrassing position. The Baukalis priest's open rejection of the authority of the Bible demanded radical surgery. Alexander knew that some form of discipline must be applied. He was also sure that extreme punishment, excommunication, would so upset the influential Baukalis congregation that such action would rock the foundations of Alexandrian society, an explosion he dreaded.

After much deliberation, he opted to steer a middle course. He informed Arius that he would be granted the privilege of administering the sacraments, but he was not to teach or preach from the pulpit until the whole matter could be brought before a synod of bishops.

In the crisis, Alexander felt the need to consult someone to help him decide what course of action to follow. He decided to go into conference with Athanasius.

The apprentice revealed a wisdom beyond his years. "Why do you not alert the churches in Egypt and Syria of the state of things?" he suggested. "You might send out a circular letter warning all true Christians to break fellowship with Christ's enemies — specifically, to be on guard against the impious doctrines of Arius."

"Excellent advice," Alexander said buoyantly. "I shall do it."

"Also, you might add a note of warning against the erroneous teachings of Eusebius of Nicodemia."

"That too," Alexander said. "I thank you, dear Athanasius. You have been a great help to me."

The archbishop secured the signatures of thirty priests and forty deacons for his encyclical letter and dispatched it to both Eastern and Western churches.

Not satisfied with verbal communications only, he overcame his fears and convened a provincial counsel made up of one hundred bishops. They came from Libya, Tripolitanica, and Pentapolis for the express purpose of trying Arius for heresy. They met in the Church of St. Theonis in the Egyptian quarter of Alexandria. It was the summer of 323. Alexander presided. The first step he undertook was to call on Arius to give a brief statement of his creed.

Arius rose, took his place behind the pulpit, and faced the court. He was aware that he was confronting an unfriendly audience. Nevertheless, it was with the utmost self-assurance that he read the summary of his views:

"I believe that God was not always a Father, but there was a time when He was only God and was not a Father. I believe that afterward He became a Father and that the Son was not always such.

"I believe that there is a Trinity, but the persons of the Trinity are not all alike in majesty. Their substances are unmingled with one another, the Father being immensely more glorious than the Son. The Father, being without beginning, is as to His essence different from the Son; that, in short, the Father is invisible, ineffable, and incomprehensible to the Son; and that it is evident that that which had a beginning, namely, the Son, can never thoroughly comprehend the nature and quality of that which is without a beginning, namely, the Father.

"I believe that the Son is not eternal nor coequal with the Father nor begotten together with the Father nor has the same being with him, as some affirm."

"I should like to ask you," Alexander said, fixing his eyes on the priest, "do you believe that the Son of God was created?"

"I believe He was created," Arius replied. "I believe He was the first of all created beings and in that sense He is the only begotten of the Father. He was created after the image of the Divine Wisdom and therefore called the Word. He is incapable of thoroughly knowing the Father's nature or His own."

"A final question," Alexander said, fighting to keep his temper under control. "Do you believe that Jesus was capable of changing from good to evil?"

"I believe Jesus was able to change from good to evil," Arius answered.

"That will do. You may be seated."

Alexander turned to address the council, most of its members by now in a state of semishock. "You, my brethren, have heard the pronouncements of this ordained priest." He pointed to Arius. "Will all who are convinced that this man's doctrines are unscriptural and therefore heretical raise the right hand."

Almost every right hand shot up.

"As far as I am able to discover, everyone present has so signified," Alexander said. "If I am mistaken, will any of you convinced that the doctrines to Arius are *not* heretical please raise the right hand."

Slowly two hands went up.

"Will you who have raised your hands please rise," Alexander said.

Two bishops struggled to their feet.

"Secundus and Theonis, do I understand that you are in agreement with the teachings of Arius?"

"We are," they said.

"Very well." Alexander, speaking in a solemn voice, said, "Arius, Secundus, Theonis, it is my sad duty to announce that this council has voted almost unanimously to condemn your doctrines as counter to the Word of God and therefore heretical. In the light of Paul's injunction, 'Though we, or an angel from heaven, preach any other gospel than that which we have preached unto you, let him be accursed,' this council hereby officially invokes the anathema of Almighty God on you . . . and on your teachings. Furthermore, until you do repent of your sins and publicly repudiate your errors you are relieved of all your clerical duties. This session is adjourned."

It was anticipated by Alexander and Athanasius that Arius would accept the judgment with bad grace. And so it was. Like an ambitious politician, Arius went from door to door through the streets of Alexandria, pleading with its residents to demand of Alexander a new trial at which he would be exonerated and restored to full powers.

It was at this point that Emperor Constantine became fully aware of the developments in Alexandria and was drawn, against his will, into the controversy.

Chapter 5

Nicea, the "City of Victory" (so designated by Lysimachus, former king of Macedonia), straddled a strip of territory bordering Lake Ascania. Historians ranked Nicea the second city in importance in the province of Bithynia. It was, therefore, a strategic center for a church council. Roman citizens generally applauded the action when Emperor Constantine selected Nicea for the holding of the convocation.

Lysimachus had directed his contractor to build the original city four square. He carried out the assignment to perfection. The result was that Nicea stood out as a creation admired for its elegance and the symmetry of its architecture, a thing of rare beauty. The excellent site was to represent the focal point where the issue between orthodoxy and Arianism would find a solution, as Constantine hoped, once for all.

Sessions were scheduled to be held in the largest hall in the imperial palace, a spacious chamber tastefully laid out. Here were arranged ivory seats marked for the bishops and wooden chairs for presbyters and deacons. The hall was patterned in the form of an amphitheater, with a wide podium stretching across its front. On a table next to the golden throne, the centerpiece, there was a copy of the four Gospels, indicating the authority to which all appeals would be made in matters of controversy. Along the walls of the auditorium, torches encased in bronze holders had been spaced at regular intervals, these to furnish lighting for the evening meetings. High at the rear and on either side hung balconies overlooking the floor. These facilities were open to spectators who wished to audit the debates.

Constantine had generously agreed to defray the traveling expenses as well as the cost of lodging and meals of the delegates. Each delegate was attended by three slaves. Approximately two thousand bodies swarmed into Nicea, to the delight of the innkeepers and restauranteurs.

The council convened on June 14 of the year 325. It extended two months and ten days. Constantine had just entered the thirteenth year of his rule and was at the zenith of his popularity and power.

The 328 commissioners who crowded into Nicea from all parts of the empire added up to an interesting spectrum of personnel. There was the bearded and emaciated Paphnutius, a Coptic hermit who had lost an eye in one of the persecutions, a character so revered that Constantine, it was reported, had kissed the eyeless socket. There was the learned Eusebius of Caesarea, ecclesiastical historian, fanatically loyal to Constantine and known to tilt toward Arianism. There was the Syrian deputy Eustathius, fully committed to orthodoxy. There was Macarius, conservative bishop of Jerusalem. There was Paul of NeoCaesarea, whose paralyzed hands bore silent witness to the torture he had endured under Diocletian. From Cappadocia in Asia Minor came Leontius, supposed to have possessed the extraordinary gift of prophecy. Present too was Eusebius, a celebrity from Nicodemia, stout defender of the Arian position and very much of an influence on Constantine and his family. There was James of Nisibis; in his lifetime he had been routed from his home and forced to live in mountainous caves. There was Caecilian, reputable bishop from Carthage, the stalwart leader whom the Donatists had opposed ever so bitterly. There was Marcellus of Ancyra, a giant of a man and vigorous challenger of Arius. There was Spyridion, the eccentric shepherd-bishop from Cyprus, credited with the ability to perform miracles. There was Theophilus the Goth, teacher of Ulphilus, successful Arian missionary to the Visigoths. There was the saintly Hosius, bishop of Cordova, personal counselor of Constantine, called by the historian Eusebius "world-renowned Spaniard." There was Acesius, the Novatian, to be marked for prominence; when Constantine later asked him why he was not in communion with the church and received no answer, he was targeted with the emperor's stinging, "Take a ladder, Acesius, and climb up by yourself to heaven." There was the venerable Alexander of Alexandria, accompanied by young Athanasius the archdeacon, full of fire and enthusiasm, destined to assume a major role in the discussions.

Of the delegates present, numerically the orthodox party, holding tenaciously to the doctrine of the full deity of Christ, constituted the minority. Next was the Arian wing, by far the most vocal. Finally, the Semi-Arians, or moderates, representing the majority, numbered as many as the other two divisions together.

There was a reason for this. Not a few moderates took the middle ground either because they entertained conservative instincts but lacked doctrinal discernment or because they held no firm convictions and so were easily swayed by the rhetoric of the noisiest speakers.

One prominent feature of the assembly was never known, not even suspected, by Emperor Constantine or by any of the commissioners: the Council of Nicea would one day be recognized as a landmark, a turning point in the history of the Christian Church. Who would have imagined that the fruit of its deliberations, the Nicene Creed in its refined form, would eventually be recited from Lord's Day to Lord's Day in many civilized countries in the world? From the tiny acorn of Nicea there would spring a mighty oak which was to spread its boughs to provide inspiration and encouragement for believers from every tongue, kindred, tribe, and people.

Yet if the Nicene fathers were in darkness with reference to the future, they were very much aware of a present dimension of the counsel. To a man, they knew and rejoiced with joy indescribable that Nicea pointed up a profound change in the relation of state to church. Until Constantine, the emperors at Rome, especially tyrants like Nero and Diocletian, had sought resolutely to stamp out the Christian faith. It was Constantine, for all his eccentricities and inconsistencies of character, who, in the providence of the Almighty, would transform the nightmare of bitter hostility into the sweet dream of peace and tolerance. And for this, every bishop, presbyter, and deacon in the conference would joyously write his name on the roster of the mythical Hall of Fame.

Chapter 6

The father of Constantine, Constantine Chlorus, officiated as co-emperor (with Galarius) for a brief time. Galarius died prematurely, leaving the living partner in full control. Since Constantine Chlorus had earlier in his life served as a general in the Roman army, it was natural that his son should take up a military career. Constantine attained distinction during the Roman wars with Egypt and Persia.

On the death of his father, Constantine was made emperor. Immediately a general named Maxentius came forward to challenge his right to the imperial purple. Constantine, at the head of an army of almost one hundred thousand troops, met and soundly defeated the challenger at the Milvian Bridge near Rome. In despair, Maxentius threw himself into the Tiber River. Constantine and his men marched triumphantly into Rome to be received by a wildly cheering public.

Early in the evening, before the battle was joined, Constantine claimed he had been caught up in a trance and beheld a phenomenon which, he asserted, changed his life. While peering in the sky, he noticed a shining cross quivering above the sinking sun. Over the sun appeared the words "By this sign conquer." This he interpreted to mean that he would triumph over Maxentius in the conflict. He told his soldiers that Christ had also come to him and directed him to make a standard in the form of a cross and with it proceed against the foe. Henceforth, Constantine resolved, the crucifix would be affixed to the shield of his soldiers, thus displacing the insignia of the eagle with the cross.

Upon his promotion to the highest honor in the land, Constantine issued an edict of toleration granting freedom to all forms of worship, particularly those related to Christianity. Also, he ordered all confiscated church property restored. He exempted the clergy from military duty, facilitated the emancipation of Christian slaves, contributed liberally to the support of bishops, enjoined the civil observance of Sunday as a day of special worship, gave his children a Christian education, and diligently attended church services.

Yet, if the new emperor metaphorically emerged from the grave, alas, he still wore stained grave clothes. In the very year he convened the Council of Nicea, he ordered the execution of his brother-in-law, Licinius, ostensibly for political reasons. Without justification, he also had the eleven-year-old nephew of Licinius slain. One year after the termination of the Council of Nicea, he murdered his oldest son, Crispus, whom he suspected of committing adultery, but without evidence and without a trial. Moreover, he continued the practice of consulting soothsayers. He retained the title Pontifex Maximus, high priest of the pagan hierarchy. Roman coins, with his approval, bore the name of Christ on one side and Sol Invictus, the title of the sun god, on the other.

In brief, all evidence points to the fact that Constantine was more concerned with favoring the social and civil aspects of the Christian faith than supporting its evangelical and missionary thrust. Throughout the final years of his life, he was alternately praised and presented by both Christians and heathen, by Arians and the orthodox, as they found him either supporting or condemning, according to his whim. He postponed the rite of baptism until his deathbed. What was written of Jacob's son Reuben, of Old Testament vintage, might well be said of Constantine: "Unstable as water . . ."

The hour arrived for the Council of Nicea to start. The emperor made his entrance into the great hall. At a given signal, the delegates rose and faced His Majesty. They had expected him to present himself surrounded by a cadre of guards. To their surprise, the unpredictable monarch came alone. He projected an impressive figure. Tall, slender, arrayed in a robe of rich purple and wearing a diadem of gold, he moved slowly down the central aisle, bowing to his subjects on the right and on the left. His dark eyes sparkled, his handsome features, marred only by a slight goiter on the throat, were aflame with pleasure.

He reached the podium and turned and spread his hands, indicating that the commissioners were to be seated. He then ascended the golden throne and seated himself.

Eusebius of Caesarea rose and, in a style of blank verse, read a poem of praise, eulogizing his emperor for his sensational victory over his enemy at Milvian Bridge. When he had finished,

Constantine stood and, in a prepared address, delivered in Latin the words:

> *It is my highest wish, my friends, that I might be permitted to enjoy your assembly. I must thank God that, in addition to all other blessings, he has shown me the highest one of all: to see you all gathered here in harmony and with one mind. May no malicious enemy rob us of this happiness, and after the tyranny of the enemies of Christ (Licinius and his army) are conquered by the help of the Redeemer, the wicked demon shall not persecute the divine law with new blasphemies. Discord in the church I consider more painful than any other war . . . When I heard of your divisions, I was convinced that this matter should by no means be neglected, and in the desire to assist by my service, I have summoned you without delay. I shall, however, feel my desire fulfilled only when I see the minds of all united in that peaceful harmony which you, as the anointed of God, must preach to others. Delay not therefore, my friends, delay not, servants of God; put away all causes of strife, and loose all knots of discord by the laws of peace. Thus shall you accomplish the work most pleasing to God, and confer upon me, your fellow servant, an exceeding great joy.*

Constantine resumed his chair. He then produced a number of recriminatory letters he had received and explained that both sides had sent him communications couched in bitter terms accusing fellow clergymen with unfair charges. This, he said sternly, he would not tolerate. He had a servant bring on a brazier stoked with live coals. He took the letters and burned every one, while urging all in his presence to exercise brotherly love and charity.

After that, he had the assembly rise. He announced that the business of the body would begin on the morrow and, following a brief prayer, dismissed the councilmen.

Chapter 7

The first day was restricted to an executive session, or private meeting, the public being excluded from the hearings. Hosius, the moderator, called on Arius to come forward. He said to the priest, "You are now granted the opportunity to state your concept of the person of Jesus Christ. I exhort you to be forthright and come to the point without an excess of rhetoric."

Pale, but completely composed, Arius stood facing the council, a profile of self-confidence. In a clear, resonant voice, he again spelled out his views of Jesus. He reiterated his conviction that Christ was the first of all created beings. Since he was the Son, it followed that the Father must have preceded him in the framework of the temporal. Therefore there had to be a time when Jesus had no previous existence. Arius insisted that his understanding of the nature of the Son, despite allegations to the contrary, was in actuality representative of the historic, traditional position of the Catholic church.

He went on to read excerpts from his book, *Thalia*. The assertions in it so patently contradicted the New Testament teaching concerning the divine nature of Christ that some of the commissioners stopped their ears and cried out in protest.

No action was taken during the executive session.

Hosius declared that since Arius's speech had set the stage for the formal debate, there would be no more items of business under consideration that day except to discuss the general format of the proceeding sessions.

On the second morning, the delegates came together to take up the real matter at hand. The public was permitted to attend and filled the balcony to overflowing.

As is sometimes the case when ecclesiastics assemble to transact church problems, no sooner had Hosius called the council to order and prayed than confusion reigned. In religion, as in politics, preconception and prejudice too frequently displace calm, deliberate reflection. A personal witness of the early Nicene sessions labeled the debaters "a set of demoniacs driven by evil forces and malignant passions."

████, of course, a literary overkill fired off by an unsympathetic observer. Nevertheless, it is true that the opening chapters of the story of Nicea were not sprinkled with beams of sweetness and shafts of light. A cross section of the churchmen present had not received training in the catechetical classrooms of Alexandria or in the schools of jurisprudence of Rome or on the stoa (porches) in Athens where philosophers held sway. There were moments when an undiscerning delegate would interrupt a speaker by loudly posing a question or questions. Occasionally a jester might fracture the assembly with a subtle jibe or joke. Again, it would happen that after a gifted commissioner had articulated his point in a burst of oratory, the house would reverberate with shouts of approval.

Gradually, however, as the days slipped by, the patient Hosius, through the learning process (though with nothing like Robert's *Rules of Order* to go by), managed to check the disturbances. By the time August had arrived, the sessions had obtained a degree of orderliness that was a tribute to Hosius and to the other Nicene fathers.

To his eternal credit, Hosius made it plain to everyone that the principle focus of all discussion must be kept in view, namely, the framing of a comprehensive, definitive creed which had at its center the true nature of the Lord Jesus Christ. Everything else had to be secondary. Minor matters would undoubtedly be introduced but, the chairman insisted, would not be allowed to overshadow the goal for which Emperor Constantine had summoned his subjects to Nicea.

As the debate wore on, three gifted spokesmen moved into the circle of prominence: Eusebius of Nicodemia, a confirmed disciple of Arius; Eusebius of Caesarea, the historian, who leaned toward Semi-Arianism; and Athanasius, stout defender of orthodoxy.

The three made up a composite of contrasts. Eusebius of Nicodemia, a mountain of a man, clean shaven, with white flowing hair, squinty eyes, the square shoulders of an athlete, and a booming voice, had recently celebrated his fifty-fourth birthday. The scholarly Eusebius of Caesarea, the historian, ten years his namesake's junior and a close friend of the emperor, was, like Arius, stately, thin — almost to the point of emaciation — as gentle in disposition as the other Eusebius was gruff. Both, if standing beside Athanasius, would have towered above him like willow trees above a shrub. Athanasius had lately coaxed a mustache into existence, hoping that somehow it might add maturity to his boyish face.

If the trio differed in physical appearance, they had certain intellectual features in common. All were skilled in the art of dialectical reasoning. All were perfectly at home in the genre of the literary and theological and philosophical classics and quoted from them freely. All knew how to analyze the arguments of the opposition and possessed the ability to respond without falling back on a vocabulary so ponderous as to confuse the minds of the less well-instructed.

And so through July and far into August controversy swirled around one pivotal point. Strange as it may appear, the battle was not fought over one paragraph or one sentence or even one word; it raged, in fact, over one letter.

The standard-bearers of orthodoxy maintained that Jesus Christ *was*, and *is*, God in the flesh, no less. The Arians contended that Jesus Christ was *like* God. The difference lay in the two terms: the Greek word *homoousios*, meaning "of the *same* substance" — held by the proponents of orthodoxy — over against *homoiousios*, "of *like* substance" — maintained by the Arianizing opponents of orthodoxy.

The Semi-Arians felt that the spokesmen for both of the other sides were too immersed in the technical idiom to quarrel.

Why not, they said in essence, retain the simple language of the Bible and not be so concerned over definitions or interpretations?

Speaking for the toning down of a rigid creed, one of the Arians summarized this stance by stating, "Christ and his disciples left us not a system of logic of human formula but the naked truth to be guarded by faith and good word."

To this posture the combined bloc of Arian and Semi-Arians agreed heartily. By a code of secret signals and head movements, they communicated their approval.

Eusebius of Nicodemia voiced his acceptance of this position in a burst of eloquence. "What are we but men unable to understand a thousand things that lie immediately at our feet?" he stormed.

"Who knows how the soul is united with the body and how it leaves the body? What is the essence of angels and the essence of our own soul? We ought to be satisfied with the testimony of the Father respecting his Son: 'This is my beloved Son in whom I am well pleased. Hear Him.' Jesus Himself tells us what we should know concerning Him: 'God so loved the world as to send His only-begotten Son that whosoever believes in Him might not perish, but have everlasting life.' Sufficient therefore for us, in order to obtain salvation, is the faith which enables us to know the Almighty God as our Father, and to receive His only-begotten Son as our Savior." This powerful speech was followed by a round applause.

This and other persuasive speeches from the Arian delegation made a deep impression on the commissioners. Everything appeared to be pointing toward a certain victory for the liberalizing coalition.

During a lull in the war of words, a priest with sympathies toward Arianism cornered Athanasius and said to him, "Why do you not admit it? You are fighting a losing battle. Do you not know that at this moment the whole world is against Athanasius?"

The undersized archdeacon threw back his shoulders and drew a long breath. He looked straight into the face of his heckler. His probing eyes flashed like the Northern Lights as he uttered the memorable words, "Is the world against Athanasius? So be it. Then Athanasius is against the world!"

Chapter 8

The crisis in the debate came at the halfway point.

Athanasius, believing that his defense rested solely on the authority of the Word of God, claimed the floor. For proof texts in support of Christ's deity, he quoted what he felt were key passages, such as the Savior's words, "I and the Father are one." From John, "In the beginning was the Word, and the Word was with God, and the Word was God." "This one [Jesus] is the true God and eternal life." And from Paul, "In him dwells the fullness of the Godhead bodily." "Who is over all [Jesus] God blessed forever."

Promptly Eusebius of Nicodemia came back with another scriptural reference: "But did not Jesus say, 'The Father is greater than I?' What could be greater evidence that the Father is superior to the Son than a clear, unequivocal statement like this?"

Athanasius was there with a ready answer. "Jesus voluntarily took on Himself the role of the suffering Servant of Jehovah," he declared. "On this account the properties of human nature are said to be His. He knew what it meant to be hurt, to thirst, to hunger, and the like, of which the flesh is capable. Like Jacob, He knew what it meant to be consumed in the day by drought and frost by night; to have sleep depart from His eyes; to weep; to ask; to flee; and to deprecate the cup — in a word, to endure all that belongs to human frailty. But we must — we *must* keep in mind that He experienced all these vicissitudes in His office of Mediator. They in no wise contravene the other side of His true nature, which, like the Father's, is unassailably divine."

Eusebius was on his feet. "Still, is it not true that Jesus is said to be 'the firstborn of all creation?' Must we then, in the ordinary sense of the term, not properly understand him to have been created?"

"No!" Athanasius thundered. "Eusebius is falling back on the wicked device of setting one part of Scripture over against another. This is the method of the devil himself. In the expression 'the firstborn of all creation,' the sacred writer is showing that the Son of God is *other* than the whole creation and not a creature. In Jewish custom, it was the portion of the elder brother, or firstborn, to inherit everything the father bequeathed to him. So it is with Jesus, our elder brother. He has only to ask the Father, and the Father will bestow on Him the nations for His inheritance and the uttermost parts of the earth for His possessions. Now if He is a creature, He will be the firstborn of Himself because He is said to create 'all things.' How, then, is it possible to be before and after Himself? If He is a creature and the whole of creation through Him came to be and in Him consists, how can He create the creation and be one of the things which consists of Himself?"

It was at this juncture that the current began to turn in favor of orthodoxy. The Arianizers, aware of the trend away from their tenets, decided compromisingly to put together a creed that would satisfy the conservatives and at the same time give themselves an opening to interpret declarations their own way.

Eusebius of Caesarea presented their creed:

> *We believe in one God, Father Almighty, Maker of all things, visible and invisible, and in one Lord Jesus Christ, the Word of God, God of God, Life of Life, the only-begotten Son, firstborn of every creature, begotten of the Father before all ages, by Whom all things were made; Who for our salvation was incarnate, and lived among men; Who suffered and rose again the third day, and ascended to the Father, and shall come again in glory both to judge the quick and the dead. We also believe in the Holy Ghost. Each of them we believe to be and to subsist — the Father truly Father, the Son truly Son, the Holy Ghost truly Holy Ghost, as our Lord when He sent forth His Apostles to preach said, Go and make disciples of all nations, baptizing them in the name of the Father, and of the Son, and of the Holy Ghost.*

Athanasius promptly challenged the creed. He accused Arius and his followers of holding mental reservations. He backed his allegation by citing an excerpt from *Thalia* where Arius categorically denied that Jesus is God.

The Arians came back by assuring the men of the council that they could freely accept the terms *God*, *image of God*, and *power of God* as applied to Christ. The giveaway, however, surfaced when one of their party advised the assembly that they believed it was "*the right of every delegate to interpret these and other terms according to his own private point of view.*"

The saber-sharp mind of Athanasius penetrated what he designated "the evasive ingenuity of the Arians." He held up a copy of a letter written by Eusebius of Nicodemia in which the bishop asserted that he and the followers of Arius could never declare Christ to be "uncreated." Athanasius said crisply, "This is a blatant denial that Jesus is 'the Son of God, of one substance with the Father.' "

Archbishop Alexander, who previously had encouraged Athanasius to do the lion's share of the debating, stood to his feet and said, "There is a significant omission in the statement read by our brother Eusebius. I listened in vain for the use of the word *homoousios*, 'of the same substance' — that is, of the same substance the Son bears to the Father. This is the heart, soul, and kidneys of the whole of our Christian heritage. Without it, there is no salvation."

The disputation continued with considerable heat. Athanasius scored heavily when he pointed out that the atonement, or Christ's offering Himself on the cross in the place of sinners, was valueless apart from his deity. He said:

> *At His death, marvelous to relate, or rather at His triumph over death — the cross, I mean — all creation was confessing that He who was made manifest and suffered in the body was not man merely, but the Son of God and the Savior of all. For the sun hid his face, and the earth quaked and mountains were rent, and all men were awed at the happening. Now these things show that Christ on the cross was God, and all creation His slaves. By the offering unto death the body He Himself had taken was an offering and a sacrifice free from any stain, it proves to us that straightway He put away sin by the sacrifice of Himself, the divine-*

human Equivalent. Thus He, the incorruptible Son of God, joined with all of a like nature, clothed us all with incorruption by the promise of a resurrection. Without these truths our faith is vain and our message a hollow mockery.

From this proposition, Athanasius concluded that it logically followed that because of this redemption wrought by Christ, the ground of salvation did not rest in works righteousness but strictly on the merit of Jesus's unimpeachable righteousness and suffering at Calvary.

Chapter 9

In the process of time, a committee chaired by Athanasius drew up a creed and then presented it to the council for acceptance or rejection. This is the fruit of the committee's labors:

> *We believe in one God, Father Almighty, Maker of all things visible and invisible; and in one Jesus Christ, the Son of God, begotten of the Father, only-begotten, that is, of the essence of the Father, God of God, and Light of Light, very God of very God, begotten, not made; of one essence with (homoosios) the Father; by whom all things were made, both in heaven and in earth. Who for us men and our salvation came down, and was incarnate, and was made man; suffered, and rose the third day; ascended into the heavens; shall come to judge the quick and the dead.*

All the members of the council except five signed the document. Seventeen others hesitated for a time. They might not have subscribed but for the pressure put on them by Constantine. The emperor, after considerable vacillating, was persuaded that the new creed was the right one. He earnestly pleaded with the wavering commissioners to affix their signatures. Even Eusebius of Nicodemia, the last of the holdouts, finally gave in and endorsed the creed, principally, he admitted to his friends, for the sake of peace.

Constantine promptly ordered those who had balked at the contents of the creed sent into exile. Arius and two bishops, Secundus and Theonas, together with two deacons who refused to conform, were deposed and banished to Illyricum, a bleak stretch of territory on the Balkan Peninsula.

Constantine then ordered all the books of Arius burned.

The council then took up other items of business of less importance. By early August, the bulk of the work was concluded, much to the relief of Constantine and all others present.

Before the delegates returned to their homes, the ruler invited all to a magnificent banquet held in the dining room of the imperial palace. After the dinner, the emperor opened a cornucopia of gifts and pressed them on his guests. In addition, he lavished large sums of money to be distributed to various charitable foundations.

Full of geniality (and probably sweet wine), Constantine rose from the table and offered an address. In it he counseled his hearers to bury party strife and intolerance. Rather, he urged them to buy peace at all costs, to love truth, and to keep their minds free from the stain of prejudice. He engaged in a lengthy, rambling speech during which most of his subjects waged a losing struggle against sleep.

He concluded with the words, "I too am a bishop. You are bishops for matters within the church, and God has made me a bishop for things without."

He ordered a report of the creed circulated in Egypt, Pentapolis, and Libya. He also sent letters to officials in all sections of the empire with this explanation:

The three hundred and more church officials who have been meeting in Nicea have declared that there is only one faith, the same everywhere, which alone is conformable to the truths of the divine law, and that the egregious Arius appears to have been the victim of the power of the devil. But now all divisions, schisms, disturbances and fatal poisons of discord have, by the will of God, been overruled by the refulgence of the truth.

Certainly the importance of the creed is inestimable. But, like a ferryboat when approaching a wharf strikes against the bulwark from side to side until finally grooved, the product of Nicea would have to be refined by more Christian councils before it was to become the fulfillment of the archdeacon's prediction.

Soon after the close of the assembly, Eusebius of Nicodemia and a number of other bishops repudiated their endorsement of the creed and demanded that their names be removed from the list of subscribers. And while the orthodox segment of the council was rejoicing over its smashing victory at Nicea, Eusebius, who had gained firm control of the eastern segment of the church, was quietly working out a plan to destroy Athanasius.

There lived in Alexandria a proud bishop named Meletius. This man had suffered imprisonment at the hands of Diocletian, the last of the Roman emperors to persecute Christians violently. On his release from prison, Meletius began to strut the boards of the ecclesiastical stage. Insolently he challenged the authority of Archbishop Alexander and, on his own initiative, practiced ordaining other bishops.

Curiously, this sixty-year-old martinet and his followers loudly proclaimed their orthodoxy. They paid lip service to the truthfulness of the Nicene Creed. Their profession, however, just as loudly contradicted their life-style. Petty, impatient, headstrong, they fitted the description of the questionable friends of Job. Of these three, Job said with blistering sarcasm, "No doubt you are the people and wisdom shall perish with you." And like Job's "comforters," the Meletians were great proponents of freedom — they granted liberty to everyone who agreed with them!

Before the Egyptian bishops were able to take disciplinary action against Meletius, Eusebius of Nicodemia courted the friendship of Meletius and his coterie by utilizing political maneuvering and flattery. The fusing of the two factions was bizarre. Between them no natural love existed. Yet in their common hatred of Athanasius, they discovered a bond that induced them to bury their differences and braided them together in a token alliance.

Aware of the merger, Athanasius likened it, doubtlessly, to the union of King Herod and Roman Proconsul Pilate, the New Testament odd couple. Until Christ appeared on the scene, the two had been political foes. On the day they encountered the Savior face-to-face, they became friends.

The Council of Nicea had done two things to catapult Athanasius into a place in the sun. First, it marked him out as a leader of men. People from the remotest sections of the empire heard reports of his stirring speeches at Nicea. And those in the council could not but acknowledge his God-bestowed gifts, his passionate devotion to Christ, his remarkable grasp of Biblical doctrine, and his boldness in the face of opposition.

Second, the conflict with the Arians had made him a target for their abuse. From Nicea on, he was destined to be the object of vilification, scorn, and persecution, with the specter of death lurking around the curve of every road. Until Athanasius's death, the Arians would reckon him to be public enemy number one.

Chapter 10

Following the passing of godly Alexander, the Christians of Alexandria clamored for the ordination of Athanasius as his successor. His situation corresponded precisely to that of two of his contemporaries, Augustine of Hippo and Ambrose of Milan. Both of these renowned laymen had been forced against their wills to accept the bishop's surplice.

Athanasius held out against pressures as long as he could. Finally, on the strength of Paul's admonition, "Submitting yourselves one to another in the fear of God," with a heavy heart he gave up and yielded to the power of public opinion. On June 8, 326, he was consecrated to the post of the Archbishop of Alexandria.

At once the Arians brought out their heavy artillery. Through their spokesman, a priest named Philostorcus, they swore that the ordination service had been conducted secretly in a dark corner of the Cathedral of St. Dionysius. Moreover, the accusers said, subsequent to the ordination, the Synod of Alexandria had censured Athanasius for permitting such an outrageous and unethical ceremony to be performed.

But the trumped-up version of the ordination service was corrected almost as soon as it was publicized. The Egyptian bishops met in a special synod and voted unanimously to vindicate Athanasius. They also approved the action of the churchmen who had officiated at his service of consecration.

In the years following his elevation to the great honor thrust on him, Athanasius attained a dangerously heady level of prestige. Not a few of his admirers began virtually to idolize him. Gregory of Nazianzen, a dear friend, went as far as to write: "The Head of the Alexandrian Church is the Head of the World."

It was an inexcusable extravagance. Athanasius rejected the panegyric. He wrote Gregory, dressing him down in no uncertain terms.

Nevertheless there was a modicum of truth in the tribute. Athanasius now possessed the power to lift the ban on exiled heretics or deny their recall. He also had the authority to endorse the consecration of bishops and deacons. And church officials from far and near were increasingly consulting him on matters of doctrine and polity.

The Arian-Meletian coalition, not discouraged by their failure to undermine Athanasius, struck a second time. It induced three Arian deacons into requesting an interview with Constantine. They were successful. Feigning righteous indignation, the trio faulted Athanasius for usurping the authority of the imperial government in imposing tax on the public; the funds, they said, were to be used for the purchase of the linen tunic, or *stachris*. The *stachris* was worn by the priest while ministering in the sanctuary.

Constantine set a time for the trial. As matters turned out, on that date the three deacons were significantly absent from court. Two priests from Alexandria appeared in Athanasius's defense and ably refuted the charge. They vowed that Athanasius had never presumed to impose any such burden on society. Constantine ruled the indictment baseless and tossed it out of court. Other friends of Meletius launched a more serious attack. Certain false witnesses went to Constantine, complaining that Athanasius had attempted to bribe a high government official, Philumenus, offering to slip him gold if he would initiate a revolt against the emperor. The collusionists were unable to produce a scintilla of evidence to support their accusation. Athanasius, acting as his own lawyer for the defense, readily disproved the testimony. Constantine sent him back to Alexandria from Nicodemia with a letter to the churches exonerating him. This conspiracy, like the others, fell under its own weight.

Frustrated and still burning with anger because of their failures to unseat the archbishop, the Meletians informed Constantine of yet another violation of an ecclesiastical rule. They said that while visiting a small church in Mareotis, a suburb of Alexandria, Athanasius had been guilty of committing a sin — a sin of omission, but nevertheless a very grievous wrong. He had directed one of his priests, Macaris, to bring before him for questioning another priest, one of doubtful status, Ischyras. Ischyras had never been formally ordained to the priesthood and had no right whatever to be performing priestly duties, a practice he had been following without the knowledge of Athanasius.

Now Ischyras begged to be excused from reporting to Athanasius because of an illness. So Macaris, the Meletians reported to Constantine, had broken into the local church sanctuary during the serving of the Eucharist, overturned the communion table, and shattered the chalice containing the sacramental wine. This proved that Athanasius had to be guilty of sacrilege since he was responsible for the acts of his priests.

Athanasius swiftly traveled to the palace of Constantine. He had no trouble setting the record straight. There was, he pointed out, no church building in the village and therefore no church sanctuary. Actually, the tiny congregation met for worship not in a church but in the home of an orphan, Ision. How then could the breaking of a communion cup have taken place in a nonexistent sanctuary? Also, Athanasius said, his accusers were proving too much. The action they focused on occurred on a weekday. But the Eucharist was administered only on Sunday. The discrepancy was too stark to be credible. Moreover, since Ischyras was not a legally ordained priest, what justification was there for his functioning in that capacity? It was clearly a breach of church law.

Athanasius again carried the day. Once more he returned home in triumph, again bearing a communication from Constantine commending him to the churches of Egypt. "I have received your bishop Athanasius with a large measure of humility," Constantine wrote. "And treated him as a man of God."

More than ever embittered by loss of face and over the breakdown of their schemes to ruin Athanasius, his antagonists now aimed straight for his jugular vein.

In that day, the iniquity of all iniquities, the great evil that stirred excitement, passion, and prejudice among people was the practicing of sorcery. The Arians and the Meletians knew this. So they plotted to create a situation which would involve Athanasius in that next-to-unpardonable sin. They persuaded an Egyptian bishop, John Arcaph, an Arian, to send a letter to Constantine telling him that Arsenius, bishop of Hypsele, had mysteriously disappeared and that he, John Arcaph, knew on reliable authority that Athanasius had deliberately committed the murder.

The informer paraded up and down the streets of Alexandria carrying in his arm a wooden box, open at top, to display a black, withered hand. "Look!" Arcaph cried out. "This is the hand of Arsenius. Athanasius poisoned him, and the remains are being used for magical incantations."

By this time Constantine was becoming more and more irked because of the multiplicity of judgment cases the enemies of Athanasius were thrusting on him. He would gladly have brushed aside the latest indictment against the archbishop but for the fact that the charge of sorcery was too serious to be overlooked. He therefore commanded Athanasius to journey to Antioch in Syria, there to stand before the judgment seat of Censor Dalmatius, the emperor's half brother, to answer the charge.

What next unfolded contained the ingredients of a real cloak-and-dagger story.

Chapter 11

Before obeying the summons to court, Athanasius decided to lay the groundwork for the trial by engaging in a bit of detective work. He sent one of his deacons, Helias, to track down the missing Arsenius. The deacon learned that his quarry was hiding out in a monastery in Ptemencyris, on the east bank of the Nile River in Upper Egypt. He started for the town.

Meanwhile, the abbot of the monastery, Pinnes, sympathetic with Arianism, got wind of Helias's approach. Quickly he smuggled Arsenius out of the village on a river boat.

Since Pinnes was accessory to the misdeed, Helias, on the authority of Athanasius, took the collaborator into custody and escorted him to Alexandria. There, under pressure, the truth came out. Pinnes admitted that he had cooperated in the conspiracy. Arsenius, he said, was alive and healthy. Pinnes thought he had been taken to the city of Tyre but was not too sure.

The discovery of Arsenius came about as a result of a curious and unexpected chain of events.

In Tyre one evening, two servants of a magistrate in the consular service chanced to drift into an inn to enjoy a libation. While there, they overheard the name of Arsenius mentioned. From their previous conversations with their master, they had learned that Arsenius was wanted for questioning. They listened attentively, picked up word of his whereabouts, and hurried to the consul with the information.

The magistrate lost no time in getting to the hideout. He arrested Arsenius and conducted him to the residence of Paul, bishop of Tyre. Paul, a loyal friend of Athanasius, after much quizzing, drew out the needed confession. Arsenius, he told Paul, had accepted a role in the plan to downgrade Athanasius.

The upshot of the episode was that the case did not go to court. Athanasius scored an impressive moral victory. Both Arcaph and Arsenius expressed sorrow and remorse for their disgraceful conduct. Constantine breathed a high sigh of relief that the wretched business was over. The frustrated Arians and Meletians retired from the scene to stop the bleeding.

It was at this time that Constantine transferred the capital of the empire from Nicodemia to the city of Constantinople.

During the next few years, Athanasius passed some of the most enjoyable periods of his career. He occupied his days with writing, preaching, counseling, penning letters, and carrying out pastoral duties. He also took time out to visit the Christian hermits and monks inhabiting the desert. This hiatus turned out to be the calm before the storm.

The greatest mind in all the world once announced that the children of this world are wiser in their generation than the children of light. Not only so, but as history will attest, the children of this world are frequently more zealous than the children of light.

When the enemies of Athanasius calculated that the time was ripe, they regrouped and again took up the cudgels. With the encouragement of Constantia, the sister of Constantine and an enthusiastic Arian, they set up a committee and suc-ceeded in securing another audience with the emperor. Calling upon all their cunning, they managed to convince Constantine that the exoneration of Athanasius and the unfair treatment accorded Arsenius added up to a dreadful distortion. In reality, they said, what happened represented a miscarriage of justice. The reputation of a faithful servant of Christ, Arsenius, had been severely injured. Athanasius had adroitly pulled the strings and operated his puppets. He was nothing but a vile deceiver. The proper setting for his unmasking ought to be in an ecclesiastical court, not a civil court. Should not the esteemed ruler of the empire reopen the case and have Athanasius hauled before a church synod for a thorough and unbiased investigation so that the cruel wrong perpetrated on an innocent man be made right?

Constantine reluctantly agreed.

Eusebius of Nicodemia proposed that the trial be held at Caesarea. It was a shrewd ploy. At Caesarea his cohort, the historian Eusebius, was officiating as bishop. Eusebius exercised a great deal of influence in that community.

Again Constantine went along with the proposal. He instructed Athanasius to travel to Caesarea, there to answer charges leveled against him.

Athanasius divined the motive behind the move to change the venue from Nicodemia to Caesarea. He requested his good friend Hosius to plead with Constantine to shift the trial to Tyre, where the atmosphere would be more conducive to a fair hearing. By now, Constantine, not famous for the virtue of stability, was in a state of confusion. He consented to the change, much to the disgust of the Arian-Meletian axis.

A local church was to be the site of the trial.

To the historic city of Tyre Athanasius made his way, accompanied by 47 Egyptian bishops. From the eastern church came 55 other bishops, virtually all committed to the Arian position. The ubiquitous Ischyras was also present.

Ironically, the synod, purporting to be sitting as a church body, was moderated by a military official, Flavius Dionysius, brother-in-law of the emperor and a known Arian.

Like a prisoner in the dock, Athanasius was forced to stand all through the ordeal.

Shortly before the session opened, the Egyptian bishops were dismayed to see their trusted friend and faithful priest, Macaris, dragged into the sanctuary in chains.

The aged Potammon, who attended the Council of Nicea, was overcome with grief and anger. He rose, pointed an accusing finger at Eusebius of Nicodemia, whom he suspected was the instigator of the plot, and cried out, "Do you sit there and presume to be the judge of the innocent? You and I were once in prison together. I lost an eye. How came you to get off without a scratch?"

"If you are so dominating here, so far from your district," Eusebius sneered, "it is natural that your countrymen should accuse you of arrogance — as they do."

With this strident exchange, the new trial began.

In rapid succession, the spokesman for the Arian-Meletian bloc dredged up a list of charges that had already been waived in court: the doubtful circumstances surrounding the consecration of Athanasius; his alleged presumptuous action in seeking to superimpose on society the burdensome tax for the purchase of the clerical tunics; his supposed effort to bribe Philomenus to overthrow the Constantine regime; the item of the shattered communion chalice.

One of the Egyptian bishops asked Dionysius for the opportunity to respond to the accusations. In the climate of the kangaroo court, his petition was turned down. Dionysius was adamant in his refusal.

But the climax of the case featured the most dramatic as well as the most surprising twist of the day.

The Arians and Meletians were seen smirking broadly over what was obviously to be a great victory for their cause.

Suddenly, a robed cleric walked into the church carrying the familiar wooden box with top open, revealing the shriveled hand. "This," the holder testified, "absolutely proves that Athanasius is the murderer of Bishop Arsenius."

A simulated wail of horror went up from the eastern bishops. Some threw up their arms. Still others glared at Athanasius malevolently.

The Egyptian bishops were appalled and shocked at the brazenness of Athanasius's opponents.

Only Athanasius remained serene, the eye in the hurricane.

He had executed his sleuthing well, an undertaking worthy of a professional detective. For at this point, he signaled for a servant hovering in the narthex to come on the scene. The servant appeared, leading the bent figure of a man. The head of the man was covered with a dark hood.

Athanasius left his place in the dock and stepped forward to confront the two. He extended a hand and whipped the hood from the man's face. "Look up," he said.

The man looked up.

A gasp exploded from every corner of the sanctuary.

Athanasius eyed the eastern bishops and asked, "Is this Arsenius?"

Only a few nodded, blushing.

Athanasius said to Arsenius, "Give me the box and put out your hands."

Athanasius faced the eastern bishops. "Now you see," he said, making no effort to screen the note of exultation in his voice, "Arsenius has two hands, has he not? Where is the third I am supposed to have cut off and used for purposes of magical incantation?"

A dramatic silence settled over the court.

The tired eyes of the archbishop danced mischievously. "Do you not see, my brothers" — the eyes swept the circle of faces — "do you not see that God has created man with two hands only?"

The bishops from Egypt, appreciating the humor of the situation and delighted with the turn of events, laughed uproariously.

But in the sanctuary that day, prejudice and passion intersected, unholy anger and blind hatred kissed each other. Despite the overwhelming proof that Athanasius was guiltless of any and all the indictments lodged against him, the majority of the delegates voted to have Dionysius appoint a six-member commission of inquiry with authority to probe further into the behavior of Athanasius as related to the grievances listed. The committee was directed to visit Alexandria and Mareotis, confer with the residents in an attempt to ferret out the truth, and report the findings to another called synod of bishops, together with specific recommendations.

Friends of Athanasius put forth an earnest effort to alter the verdict. Bishop Alexander of Thessalonica, a courtly gentleman respected by all for his nobility of character, appealed to Dionysius to disband the commission and rule that no further action be taken. Dionysius rejected the petition in no uncertain terms.

Athanasius quietly slipped from the church. Taking with him five associate bishops, he set out for Constantinople to interview the emperor, hoping to persuade him to nullify the actions taken at Tyre.

No sooner had Athanasius withdrawn than the majority of the delegates, against the strenuous protests of the Egyptian bishops, moved to depose Athanasius and to declare him guilty on every count.

Dionysius adjourned the session. He went to his home, wrote a detailed but slanted report of the trial, and sent it to Constantine.

The Arians and Meletians, not without loss of face for the exposure of their fraud but nevertheless gleeful that a stacked court had favored their cause, assembled in an inn to celebrate their triumph.

The commission of inquiry started for Alexandria to pursue its official task.

The Egyptian bishops departed for their homes, depressed, heartsick, and wondering what now was to become of their beloved leader.

Chapter 12

The commission of inquiry (well might it have been labeled the commission of iniquity) went first to Mareotis, where it functioned like a cog in a smooth-running political machine. Actually it constituted an *ad hoc* cabal of journeymen skilled in the art of manipulation. Whenever the deputation questioned opponents of Athanasius, it invited the most vicious slanders against the archbishop's character. At the same time, it forbade faithful bishops from bearing witness to the falsity of the charge of chalice breaking, the foisting of taxes on the public, the accusation of murder — any and all incriminations involving Athanasius.

Significantly, the prefect of Egypt, Philagrius, a fanatical Arian, stationed soldiers at the points of interview with orders to intimidate anyone who might have the courage to speak out in favor of Athanasius. So intolerable was the behavior of the soldiers that the imperial magistrates of Mareotis filed a complaint to Constantine.

In Alexandria, the same biased pattern was exhibited; except here, scenes of gross brutality punctuated the interviews. While the members of the commission of inquiry looked away, local police, obviously briefed for the action, fell on residents suspected of being loyal to Athanasius and beat them mercilessly. That evening, not a few bodies went to bed bruised and broken.

The committee wound up its assignment by forwarding a communication to the Synod of Tyre, which met in a rump session, to consider the report. The content of the report surprised no one. The commission unanimously recommended that in view of the information garnered from the people of Mareotis and Alexandria: (1) with the exception of the charge of murder, all counts against Athanasius should be pronounced valid; (2) the Meletians should be declared orthodox in doctrine; (3) Ischyras must be cleared of all charges and should be ordained to the office of bishop; (4) Athanasius ought to be unfrocked and deposed from the post of archbishop. The synod, with all possible haste, voted to approve all four recommendations. While this travesty of injustice was being enacted, Athanasius and his companions were preparing to enter Constantinople.

Constantine had personally planned the layout of the new capital. In a sense, the city was, like its founder, bifacial. In general, the surface assumed the form of a triangle. The hypotenuse stretched from northeast to southwest. The adjoining lines looped in a southwesterly direction and converged at the Acropolis. West of the Acropolis nestled a random complex of buildings: the Imperial Palace; the Hippodrome; the Forum of Theodosius; the Forum of Constantine; the Column of the Goths; and a palladium representing the center of the world, the axis from which a labyrinth of streets and boulevards fanned out. These imposing structures surrounded, as though to guard the centerpiece, the statue of Constantine. It was a column one hundred feet tall, carved out of red porphyry and anchored to a slab of gleaming white marble.

The entire composite crystallized the emperor's vision: to make Constantinople superior to Rome in splendor. All the constructions were erected to stand as lasting memorials to the greatness of the lord of the empire.

Aesthetically and paradoxically, the cathedrals and churches combined to offset the beauty of the secular monuments. After viewing the collection, an observer said that it was "a heaping up of treasures, the loot of the empire stacked up to celebrate the victory of the megalomanic, fascist-like autocrat."

The result: interstratified with the gorgeous college and screaming for attention stood the contrasting assortment of centers of worship done in bad taste and notable for the projection of such pagan divinities as Apollo, Athena, and the Discuroi, the sons of Zeus. On the head of the statue of Constantine flared a picture of the emperor holding a gold scepter in one hand and a gold cross in the other. If this dichotomy appeared puzzling to the Christians in Constantinople, it points out the confusion that afflicted the polarized mind of Constantine.

Into this colorful capital Athanasius and his friends entered. The ship they had boarded at Tyre put into the Buccoleon Harbor, a key indenting the southern rim of Constantinople. From the residents of the city the archbishop found out that Constantine was feverishly busy and would undoubtedly be in no mood to receive visitors. On the particular afternoon, he would be returning from a journey abroad. The party from Alexandria took up temporary residence in an inn near the imperial palace.

Eventually the emperor appeared, riding a royal steed flanked by bodyguards. He looked on in astonishment as the slight figure of a man, weeping as though his heart would break, sifted through the cordon of guards and seized the bridle of the emperor's horse. Enraged by the impudent act, Constantine tried to shake loose the bridle and fend off the body of the intruder.

Athanasius refused to give ground. Only then did Constantine recognize him.

"Your Highness," Athanasius said respectfully but firmly, "I need to see you and plead my cause. May I?"

"I have not the time," the emperor snapped.

"Then I want only this," Athanasius persisted. "Either convene a lawful council, or summon the members of the Council of Tyre to meet with me in your presence."

Constantine was speechless.

"God will judge between you and me," Athanasius said sternly, "since you have joined the ranks of my calumniators."

The very boldness of the primate turned out to be the instrument that moved the heart of Constantine to change his posture. Relenting, he retired to his palace and wrote a letter to the members of the Synod of Tyre:

> *I have met with Athanasius and he has told me what injustice you have done him. He and those with him looked so troubled and depressed that I felt ineffable pity for him when I realized that this was Athanasius, the holy sight of whom had once been enough to draw the very Gentiles to worship the God of all. So be assured that I shall strive with all my heart to insure that everything is made firm and stable, and that the enemies who multiply blasphemies under pretense of defending God's Holy Name are scattered, destroyed and completely annihilated.*

Consternation reigned in the camp of the Arian-Meletian alliance on hearing of the communication. The blueprints the conspirators had so carefully put together to guarantee the resignation of Athanasius seemed to be going up in flames. The majority of the members of the Synod of Tyre, frightened by the tone of Constantine's letter, went home. A self-appointed committee of six, however, opted to hasten to Constantinople to attempt to bring their ruler into line with their designs.

The men had no difficulty getting a hearing. Artfully, they bypassed every one of the previous charges laid against Athanasius. Instead, they introduced a new and more monstrous accusation. They reported to the emperor that they had uncovered a scheme hatched by Athanasius, which, if carried out, would threaten the very life of His Highness and his subjects residing in and around Constantinople as well as in Alexandria. Athanasius, they claimed, had vowed that if things were to go contrary to his will, he meant to call a strike among the roustabouts on the docks at Alexandria. The effect of this wicked trick would mean that the fleet of Alexandrian corn ships would no longer be available for the importation of precious grain from abroad. That would spell disaster to the people of Byzantium and Egypt. Famine would be the inevitable consequence.

Eusebius of Nicodemia joined the committee in support of the indictment. He pointed out that such an insurrectionary move indicated that Athanasius was going over the head of the emperor, thus superseding the authority of His Highness, a treasonable offense indeed.

A few years prior to this, a distinguished Roman philosopher, Sopater, had been suspected of committing a similar crime and had forfeited his life. Was not Athanasius equally culpable? "I swear," Eusebius said, "that Athanasius is wealthy and powerful and quite adequate for such an attempt."

The long, drawn-out controversy had by now driven Constantine to the edge of despair, of mental dysfunction. His dream of peace and unity had deteriorated into a nightmare. Like Pilate before Jesus and the frenzied mob at the tribunal of the Roman proconsul, Constantine wished to wash his hands of the whole terrible business. When Athanasius would have responded to the lie perpetrated on him, Constantine disallowed any defense.

The decision he was about to make has produced much speculation. Was it, as some have believed, framed in the interest of promoting uniformity in the Roman world? Was it governed by the increasingly influential Eusebius of Nicodemia, aided and abetted by Constantia? Was it, as a few have theorized, because he felt Athanasius would enjoy physical security away from home?

What Constantine decreed, whether from anger or fear or charity or self-interest, was to banish Athanasius to Augusta Treverorum, of Treves, the capital of Gaul. He must leave immediately.

So parted two giants who have written indelible memoirs on the scroll of history. One slipped into exile in disgrace. The other remained in Constantinople to move up to higher plateaus of fame.

They were never again to meet on earth.

Chapter 13

Athanasius reached Treves in November 327. There he was to reside for two-and-a-half years.

It is true that he went to his assigned home under a dark cloud. Rejected by his emperor, abandoned by false friends, wrenched from his labors, isolated from his beloved flock — all these factors combined to press on him a burden that would have cracked a less stalwart spirit. Yet in the years ahead, looking back, he was to realize that the banishment, grievous as were the circumstances that led to it, would yield rich returns physically, mentally, and spiritually. For Treves turned out to provide for him a hiding place from the wind, a shelter from the tempest, a river of water in a dry place, the shadow of a great rock in a weary land.

He had traveled to Treves bearing his lot with shoulders bent and a heart heavy with disappointment. He discovered the community to be a virtual paradise. Unlike fever-racked John Chrysostom, who had been deported to a lonely existence in Cucusus, a stronghold of wild beasts and cruel bandits, Athanasius was ecstatic with the beauty for which Treves was renowned.

The city bordered the west bank of the Moselle River. It was planted on a grassy plain and protected by vine-covered slopes jeweled with all kinds of fruit trees. Its classical Roman name, Augusta Treverorum, bore witness to the fact that it was the summer residence of the Caesars. For years it had served as headquarters for Roman commanders.

When the archbishop had settled in Treves, one of the first to proffer him a hearty welcome was Constantine II, the emperor's oldest son. Constantine II had supported Athanasius in his struggle against the Arians. The youth was a gracious, genteel character. Until Athanasius was to leave the city, the two would maintain the most cordial and stimulating relations.

Another source of encouragement was Bishop Maximin, a prince of the church and one blessed with distinguished gifts. Ever since Nicea, the good man had also thrown his influence behind Athanasius and all that he stood for.

With these two dignitaries functioning as tonics to his spirit and with a great deal of time for prayer, meditation, public worship, occasional preaching, and rest, Athanasius invested his time in some of his best writings. His *Festal Letters* reveal that he could be as tender in shepherding as he was polemic in controversy. They contain gems of consolation to the churches in Egypt. An example:

> *Oh my beloved and dearest, we ought not to be frightened because the world is at enmity with God. Rather let us take pains to please God under trials, which should be regarded as tests of virtue. Our Lord and Savior had worse to bear. If any of us will conform to his example, beyond doubt we shall tread upon serpents and vipers. The enemy fights against us by trials and distresses, doing all he can to overwhelm us, but the one who, with Christ's aid, prepares himself to resist, will in the end be victorious.*

During Athanasius's period of exile in Treves, two events of vast importance unfolded.

First, with the consent of Constantine, the Synod of Tyre voted to reinstate Arius and other exiled bishops. During his deportation, the priest of Baukalis had become a kind of folk hero to multitudes. Constantine sent out a circular letter to be read in the churches of Egypt. It stated:

> *We are sure that it will give you great joy to receive back the members of your own body. Great will be your pleasure. Great also will be your consolation. They are your intestines, your brothers, your fathers. You will recognize them and take them back.*

But instead of welcoming the jubilant Arius into their collective bosom, many of the citizens of Alexandria, enraged over the treatment of Athanasius and equally furious over the recall of Arius, reacted vigorously. They organized cadres of protestors. They marched through the streets of the city shouting their disapproval. Even mild-mannered monks, sojourning from their homes in the

54

desert, joined the ranks of the paraders and blended their voices with those of hundreds of laymen. Arius, frustrated, had no choice but to flee to Constantinople.

Constantine, beside himself with indignation, thought of a way to punish the Alexandrians. He commanded Alexander, the Bishop of Constantinople, to administer the Eucharist to Arius.

Alexander, a dedicated follower of Athanasius, was not of a mind to obey the direction. In anguish of soul he threw himself on the floor of the church sanctuary and tearfully prayed, "If Arius comes to the church tomorrow, Lord, take me away and let me perish with the guilty. But if Thou pitiest Thy church, as Thou hast pitied us in the past, take Arius away."

The next morning Arius was proceeding to the church, as he thought, to partake of the Eucharist. The unexpected happened.

In a letter to a friend, Athanasius described the details:

When Arius left the emperor, the Arians with their usual impetuosity, wanted to take him straight to the church. But Alexander, of blessed memory, the Bishop of Constantinople, refused permission, alleging that one who had invented a heresy ought not to be admitted to communion. Then the Arians started to threaten, "Just as a short time ago we succeeded in prevailing on the emperor to decide in favor of Arius despite you, so tomorrow Arius will join us in the Holy Communion at this church, whether you forbid it or not."

Arius, made bold by the protection of his faction, engaged in light-hearted and foolish conversation, until he was suddenly compelled by a call of nature to retire. Immediately, as it was written of another, "falling headlong, he burst asunder in the midst," and gave up the ghost, so being deprived both of communion and life.

The second event related to death as well. In the winter of 337, Constantine's robust health gave way to spells of inertia. He sought to regain his strength in hot baths, first in Constantinople, later in Helenpolis, all to no avail. Realizing he was not long for this life, like Ahithophel of the Old Testament, he set his house in order. He withdrew to Nicodemia, summoned Eusebius of that parish, and announced that he was ready to receive baptism.

The emperor then had his servants convey him to a church on a couch brocaded with white silk. Before the sacrament was administered, he discarded his purple robe, donned a spotless white garment, and received baptism. He assured all present that he was happy to die. He commended his soul to the keeping of God and drew his last breath. So passed from the earthly scene the first professing Christian emperor.

The following year, with the consent of the three ruling sons of Constantine, Athanasius was released from exile and returned to Alexandria.

Chapter 14

By the decree of the late Constantine, his firstborn, Constantine II, at the age of twenty-one, began rulership over Gaul. His second son, Constantius, at twenty, inherited Byzantium and Egypt as his portion. Constans, one year younger than Constantius, had been assigned Italy. The two older brothers had committed themselves to the teachings espoused by Athanasius; Constans became a mild Arian.

Athanasius stopped at Constantinople on his way home. He wished to pay his respects to Constantius, under whose authority he would be functioning.

When he arrived in Alexandria, the residents received him with such an outpouring of love that he was moved to tears. Demonstrations were restrained but genuine. People celebrated his homecoming with the waving of palm branches, reminiscent of Christ's entrance into Jerusalem prior to Calvary. Seated on a caparisoned donkey, Athanasius led a procession through the maze of streets. Clouds of fragrant incense billowed up from censers strung along the way. Athanasius went back to his duties fortified with fresh energy stemming from the glorious reception.

His pleasure proved to be of short duration, for trouble was brewing in the political caldron. Whereas Constantius professed to believe in orthodoxy, his personal life was nothing short of scandalous. He quickly earned a reputation as a braggart and a chronic liar. On his ascension to emperorship, he gave indication of the kind of monarch Byzantium was to have. Sated with a passion for fame but fearful lest he be deprived of his authority, he organized death squads and had them systematically wipe out all potential rivals. The purge included two of his own sons, two cousins, and an uncle, as well as the Praetorian prefect and two children of Delmatius the Censor. His rule degenerated into an era of terror.

Eusebius of Nicodemia was as successful in his power over Constantius as he had been over his father and remained as unrelenting in his opposition to Athanasius. In an interview with Constantius, Eusebius spun out new charges. Athanasius, he said, had stolen the grain which Emperor Constantine had donated to widows and children in Egypt and Libya. Moreover, on the day Athanasius had returned to Alexandria from Treves, the hypocritical archbishop had incited his henchmen to sprinkle the boulevards with the blood of the citizens, he charged.

To compound the falsifications, Eusebius asserted that Athanasius was guilty of consistently violating church law by using civil statutes to fulfill his selfish aim. This was a clear infraction of the rule laid down by Jesus Christ: "Render to Caesar the things that are Caesar's, and to God the things that are God's." That the Arians themselves were culpable of the same violation went unchallenged by the emperor.

Constantius, with the support of a synod hastily assembled at Tyre, took measures to remove Athanasius from his high position. The man whom the emperor appointed as his successor was a relatively unknown bishop named Piscus. Piscus proved to be a disaster, politically as well as intellectually. After a few weeks in office, he was dismissed summarily by order of Constantius.

Constantius then set up another bishop, an Arian, Gregory from Cappadocia. This character was a friend of the dissolute Governor Philagrius, former perfect of Egypt, who had worked diligently to support the commission of inquiry.

With the covert cooperation of the Arians, Philagrius launched a diabolical crusade against the Alexandrian Christians. Forewarned, a company of believers rushed into one of the largest churches in Alexandria, where they barricaded themselves. In order to procure material for their protection, they had to break up pews, chairs, and any article they were able to requisition.

Their efforts proved fruitless. The soldiers of Philagrius beat down the church doors, overturned the barricades, and roared into the sanctuary. They set fire to the baptistery. They proceeded to seize virgins and widows, bind their hands behind their backs, and ravish them before the horrified eyes of the male watchers. Others of the guard laid hold of the men and tried to have them deny their divine Savior. If they refused, the invaders beat them with clubs or trampled them to death. The sanctuary reverberated with lamentations heard even on the outside of the church.

While these atrocities were being carried out, Athanasius, learning of the assault, took refuge in the church of St. Theonas.

While in hiding, word reached him that Philagrius had forbidden the clergy to baptize or to visit the sick; that he had given orders to the effect that laymen must not offer prayers to God, not even in their own homes.

This development forced Athanasius to make an agonizing decision. Should he remain in Alexandria and expose himself to physical danger and probable death, or should he withdraw from the city?

Recalling the words of Christ, "When they persecute you in this city, flee to another," he interpreted the text as bearing on his particular situation. He opted to leave the city. After all, he reflected, my clerical duties are curtailed, and I cannot be of any service to my people, at least not for the present. He secured passage on a corn ship and set sail for Rome. It was his second exile, this one self-imposed.

As was to be expected, his enemies, the Arians, capitalized on the move to heap all kinds of calumny on him. He was a coward. He was a traitor to his cause. He was a miserable hypocrite, they said. He was Judas Iscariot incarnate. He forfeited all moral right to be called a representative of the Lord Christ. Athanasius accepted the denunciations patiently and found solace in prayer.

No sooner had he reached Rome when he learned to his dismay that his friend Constantine II had been ambushed and slain at Aquileia — this by the order of his younger brother Constans.

Chapter 15

Archbishop Julius, head of the Roman See, welcomed Athanasius just as Maximin had received him at Treves. Also, a gracious Christian lady, Eutropion, aunt of the three brother-emperors, opened her home on a number of occasions and warmly entertained the Alexandrian.

Athanasius was much impressed with Rome's splendor. He was filled with admiration at the sight of the massive Colosseum, the Forum, the Temple of Tarpeian, the Pantheon, and the ornate palaces occupied by the senators and consuls. He thoroughly endorsed the tribute of Horace: "It is not possible to see anything more majestic than Rome."

During his three-year residence in the Eternal City, the exile was enabled both to give and to receive, to contribute and to absorb.

To Roman society he bequeathed two important things. First, he confirmed in the minds of the Christian population the doctrines of the Trinity and the deity of Christ. The firming up of these tenets was needed. For three centuries, persecution by pagan emperors had so forced Christ's followers to struggle for survival that rare indeed had been their opportunities for intensive Bible study. Athanasius's ability to lay out profound truths with clarity and simplicity made him a popular lecturer with many hungry for a better understanding of the Bible.

Second, he succeeded in putting into perspective the misunderstood practice of monasticism. It seems that the Roman public generally nursed a dislike for Saint Anthony and his monks. Reports of certain extreme forms of asceticism had infiltrated Rome. It was natural for folk to conclude that all monks were fanatics. Athanasius assured everyone willing to listen that such was not the truth. Rather, he explained, the gentle desert dwellers, rightly or wrongly, believed they were able to serve God by spending their time in meditation, prayer, and the exercise of self-discipline.

One of the results of the archbishop's lectures was that a noblewoman of considerable wealth, Marcella, experienced a radical change in the direction of life. She became the instrument of a reformation that affected thousands of church members. Many who might be described as cardboard Christians were challenged to turn from their easygoing, complacent formalism to take seriously the words of Christ: "If anyone will come after me, let him deny himself, take up his cross daily and follow me."

Fortunately for himself, the mind of Athanasius was so constituted that it operated in a receptively reconstructive fashion. He was willing to be taught as well as to teach. As he made contact with Roman thought and culture, he could not but contrast the calm, deliberative Roman mentality with the Alexandrian inclination toward subtle mysticism, the tendency to extremism, and an insatiable thirst for novelty. Athanasius would always be grateful to the Romans for adding to his intellectual girth the dimension of solidarity.

In January 340, Archbishop Julius convened a council for the purpose of repatriating Athanasius and having him restored to his bishopric in Alexandria. Fifty Italian bishops were present. But the call issued to the Arian-minded Byzantine churchmen fell on stony soil. Realizing that the delegates were to come together as an ecclesiastical body and not under the civil aegis of Constantius, they balked. The excuse they advanced for not sending representatives bordered on the ridiculous. They said that since their emperor was locked in a war with Persia, so many impediments were blocking the highways connecting East with West that travel was rendered impossible.

To show their contempt for Julius, they staged a synod of their own at Syrian Antioch. They repeated the verdict of the Synod of Tyre, discharging Athanasius from his office as archbishop.

In addition, they formulated three creeds. The content of the creeds coincided superficially with the Nicene document. The rhetoric was ambiguous. Both Julius and Athanasius assessed the statements to add up to a cosmetic. The omission of the word *homoousios*, "of the same substance," the very pivot of the Nicene Creed, in favor of the weaker *homoiousios*, "of like substance," was significant. Constantius placed his seal of approval on the rearranged creeds.

In January 341, Eusebius of Nicodemia passed away. Coincident with his death, a tremendous earthquake shook the

Midwest. The aftershocks continued for weeks. The superstitious Emperor Constantius convinced himself that the convulsions, placed in juxtaposition with the war of attrition with Persia, was the judgment of God on him for his evil behavior. He even sold the Byzantine bishops on the notion. In contrition, the bishops met and drew up a new confession of faith as a kind of peace offering and forwarded it to Julius. It was unimpeachably orthodox.

In the interim, at Rome, Archbishop Julius went ahead with his plans to assemble the delayed council, the absence of Eastern representatives notwithstanding. Those present disposed of the business on hand very quickly. They declared Athanasius innocent of the false charges pronounced against him by the Council of Tyre. They also moved to give him the hand of fellowship, receive him into the Roman church, and grant him the full privileges of a fellow-officer.

Gregory of Alexandria dispatched a presbyter, Carpones, serving as a courier, to attempt to soften the reports of the savage treatment accorded the Alexandrian Christians. These reports, Carpones insisted, were greatly exaggerated. They originated in the camp of Gregory-haters and ought to be discounted and discarded.

The Roman bishops were not deceived. Too many witnesses of the atrocities perpetuated against Alexandrian clergy and laymen confirmed the veracity of the accounts that had been circulating the empire.

The council responded by authorizing Julius to issue a synodical letter castigating the Arians for their inhuman conduct and vindicating Athanasius for the false accusations directed against him. They also went on record as refusing to recognize the appointment of Gregory to the post of archbishop of Alexandria. That was Athanasius's exclusive honor.

Some of the friends of Athanasius communicated with Constantius and pleaded with him to cooperate with the Roman bishops in throwing support behind Athanasius and officially approving their move to return him to Alexandria. The action, implemented by the gesture of sending a copy of the Bible to the emperor, had the happy effect of mellowing Constantius's attitude toward Athanasius.

Now Constans, ruler of the Italian segment of the empire, residing at Milan, entered the picture. He sent word to Athanasius to come to his court for a private interview.

In the course of the ensuing conversation, Athanasius learned that a number of prominent western bishops had requested Constans to set up another council to make final the disposition of the archbishop's ecclesiastical status — in other words, to ratify the decision of the council held at Rome. In spite of everything that had been done, there appeared to be too many loose threads hanging in space. Why not, these bishops petitioned, hold another synod for both western and eastern bishops to wind up the whole matter? Constans consented.

It was late in the year 343. The site of the proposed council was a church in the city of Sardica (now located in Bulgaria), so designated because at that point the domain of Constans adjoined the domain of Constantius. It would be a natural meeting place. A total of 176 bishops came together — 100 from the West, 76 from the East. Hosius presided.

Whatever had been the motives of the attendants, their meeting turned into a disaster from its beginning. For immediately, pyrotechnics exploded all over the church.

The trouble began when the Arian-committed bishops from Byzantium made it clear that they would have no part in the discussion unless "they" (referring to Athanasius and his friends) were thrown out. The protesters were overruled. Hosius took the position that *all* parties present had the right to be heard and would be heard.

Visitors from Alexandria were given the privileges of the floor. They stood forth and testified that they had received unspeakable torture at the hands of the Arians. Wounds and bruises on their faces bore open confirmation of their words. They also furnished evidence showing that certain documents having governmental seals attached, scrolls which contained statements clearing the alleged persecutors of brutal behavior, were in fact downright forgeries.

At this point the eastern bishops, to a man, jumped up and stormed from the church. They retired to Philipopolis in eastern Thrace. There they constituted themselves a countercouncil. They proceeded to repeat all of the spurious accusations they had leveled against Athanasius at the Council of Tyre and voted to unfrock him. Hastily they put together another creed, carefully omitting the word *homoousios*. They dictated an encyclical letter which actually was a manifesto against Athanasius and his teachings.

Before adjourning, the Arians voted to sever the ecclesiastical heads not only of Athanasius but also of Julius, Hosius, and another Athanasius sympathizer, Bishop Protogenus.

While these fulminations were creating a hurricane at Philopopolis, at Sardica the delegation unanimously declared Athanasius guiltless of the charges against him and again moved to have him restored to his rightful office at Alexandria. At the same time, they decided to excommunicate Arian bishops who had openly denied the doctrine of Christ's full deity and, thus, in their words, "merited separation from the Catholic Church." Before breaking up, they reaffirmed their endorsement of the Nicene Creed.

The effect of the transactions made at Sardica was to generate more thunder on the left. The Arians were furious when they were given the word. They reacted with a vengeance. They asked Constantius to bear down more heavily than ever on the Christians at Alexandria. They went so far as to urge their emperor to order the decapitation of Athanasius, should he return to Alexandria.

And then a curious thing took place. It was instrumental in causing Constantius to change his attitude toward Athanasius.

The Arians persuaded Bishop Steven of Antioch, one of the leading antagonists of orthodoxy in the East, to spawn an evil plot to downgrade a fellow bishop, Euphrates, by removing him from office and deporting him to Armenia. The deed was brought to the attention of Constantius, who, it happened, was fond of Euphrates. He quickly recalled the victim from exile.

Ironically, Steven became entangled in the web of his own weaving. He it was whom Constantius ejected from his office. Steven found himself out on the street, "unwept, unhonored and unsung."

Constans, whose moral record had not been one of shining virtue, like his brother Constantius, was undergoing somewhat of a transformation in thinking and character. As a result of several interviews with Athanasius, his heart became strangely warmed toward the archbishop. To the surprise of people living near him, he was seen one Sunday to join with a large congregation in a service of worship. Christians came to the conclusion that the co-emperor was not far from the kingdom of Christ.

The truth is that Constans became so strongly convinced of the integrity of Athanasius that he wrote Constantius, entreating his brother to restore the archbishop to his post at Alexandria. In so doing, Constans unofficially endorsed the action taken by the Synod of Sardica. He went as far as to threaten his brother with civil war in the event Constantius refused to cooperate.

To the chagrin of the Arians, Constantius agreed to back Constans's position. He dispatched a message to Athanasius to return to his vacated office in Alexandria. After four years in exile, Athanasius joyfully prepared to obey the order.

Chapter 16

In February 345, the civilians of Alexandria, sick to death of the brutalities imposed by Gregory, rose in unrestrained anger and slew him. The act was unquestionably wrong. It resulted, however, in the removal of the last roadblock standing in the way of Athanasius's return to his duties.

Constantius followed his permission for Athanasius to go home with words of encouragement to him:

> *Our fixed determination is that you should continue, agreeable to our desire, to perform the office of arch-bishop in your place. May divine Providence preserve you, most beloved father, many years.*

Later he sent a second communication, filled with fresh promise. And still later, a third. He offered to provide Athanasius with a royal carriage to conduct him to Alexandria.

At the time, Athanasius was living in a suburb of Rome. He seemed in no hurry to begin his return trip. He journeyed to Treves to call on Constans, who was vacationing in that lovely city, then stopped at Rome to visit Julius.

After that, he went to Constantinople to call on Constantius. It was their third interview and was marked by the utmost cordiality on the part of the emperor. Constantius assured his guest that, as God was his witness, never again would he believe allegations against his faithful subject. All former charges initiated against him by the archbishop's opponents would be expunged from the public records. Constantius also gave his word that he would issue orders to all Egyptian magistrates to follow his example.

The exhibition of clemency is interesting in view of the tangle of developments destined to unravel. Many times Athanasius was to recall the pledges of his sovereign.

From Constantinople, Athanasius proceeded to Jerusalem, where he was given an enthusiastic welcome. A council met in a special session in order to offer greetings and congratulations because of the honors conferred on him by Constantius. Sixteen bishops subscribed their names to a synodical letter to be sent to the churches of Egypt:

> *We cannot sufficiently thank the Lord for the wonders which He works everywhere, and especially for your church, inasmuch as He restores to you your pastor and fellow-minister, Athanasius. For whoever hoped to see these things which you now enjoy? Therefore, receive him with open arms.*

In one of his later books, *The History of Arianism*, the return of the native was, he said, "A day to make men forget the past, and to strengthen them for the future." His entrance into Alexandria throbbed with such a demonstration of affection that his heart burned with indescribable joy. Throngs of men, women, and children crowded the highway to greet him, he would later say, "like the Nile in flow." Many cheered as they brandished branches of palm trees. Others spread multicolored carpets on the road. As in the homecoming after his first exile, the air was redolent with odors of rich incense. Passing through the suburbs, he could see people on the roofs of houses lifting up arms in the victory salute.

The five years that followed his return were passed quietly, uneventfully. Athanasius's bark, coming out of turgid waters, sailed serenely through open seas. He sensed that his heavenly Pilot had brought him through fire and water. His bishopric became a symbol of harmony, a rallying point for multitudes who had yearned and prayed for a cessation of hostilities. Friendly letters came in from a number of churchmen who, they claimed, had deserted him under compulsion by the Arians but who now pledged their loyal support. Two of the most influential bishops, Valens and Uracios, scholars who had opposed him at every angle, withdrew their accusations and wrote apologetic notes.

A facet of Athanasius's personality now became visible to some who had seen him in action at Nicea but knew nothing about the gentle side of his nature. In Alexandria, he strove earnestly to reconcile opposing factions, strengthen the hands of his weaker brethren, encourage the depressed, minister to the needs of the poor, and in general serve as a physician of value, healing the broken-hearted and binding up their wounds. After the crushing burdens Gregory had pressed on society, Athanasius was loved, adored, admired, all but worshiped. He was supremely happy as he looked forward to more sunny days ahead.

Then, tragically, Emperor Constans relapsed into his former iniquitous ways. He turned over the reins of his section of the empire to weak vassals, retired to Gaul, and gave himself up to riotous living. Reports of his sensuous orgies spread over the land. His behavior became a scandal and a disgrace.

One of the ablest of Constans's generals, Magnus Magnantius, took advantage of the situation. He led a revolt against the emperor and had him assassinated. Since Constans had functioned as a kind of parent-protector to Athanasius, he felt keenly the emperor's passing. He wondered how he would fare under the new administration.

Magnantius proclaimed himself co-emperor. Alarmed, Constantius promptly declared war on the usurper. Their two armies clashed at Siscia in Italy. Magnantius won an overwhelming victory over his opponent. It was, however, another instance of an army's winning the battle but losing the war. The critical conflict took place at Mursa on September 28, 351. After sickening losses on both sides, Magnantius was soundly defeated. He retreated to the Alps and, realizing his cause was lost, fell on his sword.

Constantius became the undisputed sovereign of the Roman empire. One of his first moves was to assure Athanasius that the death of Constans would do nothing to change their relations. "We have thought it good to direct our letters to you," he wrote, "exhorting you and commanding you that, as archbishop, you are to go on instructing and building up the people."

Enormously relieved, Athanasius took time in the tranquil climate of Egypt to give himself to writing. His treatise, *On the Nicene Definition of Faith*, was recognized as a masterpiece of theological exposition. In it, he first pointed out the serious errors in Arianism. He went on to show why the term *Son of God*, should be held by all who profess the true faith. He explained that the term *homoousios*, even though not found in Scripture, aptly set forth the truth of the person of the world's Savior. He closed the essay with stirring words:

Thou, beloved, on receiving this, read it to thyself, and if thou approvest it, read it also to the brethren who happen to be present, that they, too, on hearing it, may welcome the Nicene Council's zeal for truth and the exactness of its sense. . . Because to God and Father is due the glory, honor, and worship, with His co-existent Son and Word, together with the all-holy and life-giving Spirit, now and unto endless ages of ages.

The period of 351 to 355 might be described as the era of good hope for Athanasius and the Egyptian population. He rejoiced that with the help of God he was able to bring peace to his bishopric. Alas, the time frame turned out to be the calm before the storm.

Constantius succeeded in winding up the war with Persia. What followed is a commentary on the fickle character of the emperor, an almost exact copy of the dominant trait in the life of Constantine the Great, his father.

Constantius appointed as his personal counselors Valens and Uracius, the very men who had apologized to Athanasius and pledged their loyalty to him. Upon the appointment, they took off their masks and revealed their true colors. They wheeled savagely on Athanasius and heaped on him the worst kinds of epithets. They admitted their adherence to Arian doctrines. They coerced Constantius into executing a complete turnabout. With the backing of other Arian and Semi-Arian spokesmen, they persuaded their emperor to cancel the portion of grain allocated to Athanasius and have it diverted to the Arians and had Constantius issue a decree to all censors, commissioners, and bishops to break ties with Athanasius on the threat of death.

At this critical time, Archbishop Julius of Rome passed away. Another staunch Athanasian, Liberius, succeeded him. The Arians showered Liberius with communications, clamoring for him to unfrock Athanasius. This Liberius firmly refused to do.

Constantius commanded the new Roman archbishop to set up a council, the goal aimed at denouncing the pestiferous Athanasius. Liberius ignored the order.

Constantius altered his tactics. He sent Liberius a bundle of rich gifts. "I will not accept a bribe," Liberius snorted. "These are unhallowed gifts." He opened his study window and hurled the presents into the field outside the church; whereupon the emperor banished him to Thrace and appointed Felix, a deacon, in his place.

The guards of Liberius utilized every weapon in the arsenal of torture to break the prisoner: threats, complete isolation, brute force, brainwashing techniques, a wretched diet. Nothing worked.

Nothing, that is, for two years. Attrition finally wore down the sufferer. Confused, his nerves shattered, his will enfeebled, Liberius wrote Constantius under pressure, agreeing to renounce the Nicene Creed and reject the teachings of Athanasius. He was released. He died brokenhearted.

Even more pathetic was the defection of Hosius of Cordova. Now one hundred years old, with snowy hair and radiant countenance, the one often referred to as "the father of bishops," the dignitary who had moderated the councils of Nicea and Sardica, was singled out as the emperor's next target. Vainly Constantius tried to compel Hosius to recant.

The punishment was an indefinite sentence under lock and key in the dreadful dungeon of Sirmium. Once more, unspeakable methods of torture were applied. The victim was subjected to near starvation and unutterable loneliness and was bloodied, scourged, ridiculed, and whipped. The noblest of human spirits is able to endure just so much pain. Hosius finally capitulated. He signed a paper repudiating everything for which he stood.

On his deathbed, however, he took back his confession. He pronounced a sentence of judgment on the Arian creeds, reaffirmed his belief in the Nicene Creed, and departed this life joyfully, triumphantly.

Athanasius was never more magnanimous. Moved to tears over the tribulations of his beloved friends, he would not, as did some of his contemporaries, castigate them. Rather, he placed the blame for their falling away on their tormentors. He observed that the persecutors, not the persecuted, were the more responsible for the infamous action and would have much more for which to answer in the day of final judgment.

The afflictions of the two churchmen were the prelude to a torrent of hostility about to be released against the one mortal Emperor Constantius feared most: Athanasius.

Chapter 17

It was midnight, February 8, 356. In Alexandria, Athanasius was conducting a vigil service in the Church of St. Theonis, preparatory to the observation of the Eucharist the next day.

All of a sudden the stillness of the night was shattered by the tramp of marching feet. Athanasius nurtured a premonition of what was about to take place. Three weeks earlier Duke Syrianus, a Roman general, had appeared in Alexandria with a force of five thousand soldiers. He had authorized Athanasius to report to Constantius to be interviewed. Athanasius demanded to see a written order from the administration. Syrianus could not produce any such order. Athanasius, suspecting a trap, said he would not leave the city.

He was about to pay the penalty for his disobedience: arrest.

When the congregation picked up the sound of heavy footsteps without, a tremor of fear quavered through its ranks. With remarkable presence of mind, Athanasius, about to lead in prayer in the chancel, stilled the worship by stretching out his hands and calling for silence.

"Listen, my beloved, I will intone the words of Psalm 136, and you will answer antiphonally with the words 'For His mercy endures forever.'"

Thus it was that when the soldiers opened the doors and began to pour into the aisles, the words of the Psalmist rang out:

> *O give thanks unto the Lord, for He is good,*
> *For His mercy endures forever.*
> *O give thanks unto the God of gods,*
> *For His mercy endures forever.*
> *O give thanks unto the Lord of lords,*
> *For His mercy endures forever.*
> *To Him who alone does great wonders,*
> *For His mercy endures forever.*
> *To Him who by wisdom made the heavens,*
> *For His mercy endures forever . . .*

It is in the mob that human nature often descends to its lowest level of depravity. The incident of St. Theonis is a lively illustration.

As the worshipers rose from prayer, uniformed brutes fell on many with clubs and beat them mercilessly. Others tore the veils from the heads of the virgins, and if the maidens resisted they were kicked in the groin. The soldiers punctuated their savagery by mouthing horrible obscenities. This was the milder form of torture.

Other troops were busy brandishing clubs and swords with which they committed murder, slaughtering men, women, and youth indiscriminately. The pattern took on the proportions of a massacre. Cries of the wounded and dying mingled with the raucous curses of the soldiers.

Athanasius was shocked to observe Count Heraclius, envoy of Constantius, hovering in the rear of the sanctuary, patently enjoying the monstrous demonstration.

Suddenly, a detachment of soldiers seized the pews and the pulpit, together with the curtains over the windows, and, carrying the articles outside the church doors, set fire to them, adding frankincense to the flames in a spirit of amusement.

Above the welter of sounds that rocked the sanctuary, male voices called out to Athanasius, "Escape, Your Holiness! Escape! Escape!"

He was the one figure in that weird, writhing composite who retained complete composure. Too full of anger and grief to weep, he stood apart in the chancel, his lips moving in prayer.

Without warning, a curious development interrupted the holocaust. A youthful soldier sprang forward, threw himself on the throne in the center of the chancel — it was sometimes referred to as the evangelical throne — and, smirking brazenly, chanted a lascivious song in a nasal voice. He dramatized the words with suggestive motions. When he had finished, he drew from his scabbard a sabre and began to sever the throne from its moorings.

Sometime later, Athanasius would describe the strange denouement:

As if divine justice had sent the word to punish the monster, he stuck the sabre in his own bowels, and instead of carrying away the throne he drew out his own entrails by the blow. The throne took away his life.

The tragedy did not stop the carnage, but it temporarily did stay the hands of the tormentors. In the modified lull that followed the ghastly event Athanasius extended his arms, called for silence, and pronounced a benediction. For that fleeting moment, even the bloodthirsty soldiers were still.

Athanasius pleaded with the surviving Christians to make their way from the church and take with them the wounded and dying and minister aid.

A cadre of soldiers started for him, breathing out imprecations and waving their swords. Thereupon a group of brave monks fought them off while others threw a protective cordon around the archbishop. Quickly, the soldiers, anticipating the effort to escort Athanasius from the sanctuary, formed a double line between him and the door in an attempt to foil the endeavor.

At that moment, an almost surrealistic drama unfolded. The light of the church candles flickered and dimmed. The monks seized the opportunity to rescue their leader. They threw their arms around him, drew him from the chancel, and started for a side door. The scowling soldiers, restrained by a mysterious power, stood at attention without so much as raising a finger.

And so Athanasius, outwardly calm but inwardly torn asunder by the bitterness of the hour, reached the door of the church of St. Theonis, slipped outside, and melted into the winter night.

Thus began his third exile.

Chapter 18

Constantius replaced the exiled archbishop with a notorious character from Cappadocia, a rascal named George. He was reputed to be a person of savage temper, gluttonous, corrupt, illiterate. The Arians had ordained him as archbishop even before he made a profession of faith.

George promptly deposed twenty-six orthodox bishops and installed in their places a band of untrained Arian youths. He also robbed well-to-do Alexandrian citizens of their inheritance, secured a monopoly of the supplies of niter and papyrus, wrested a profit from all funerals, and permitted the deceased to be placed only in coffins manufactured by a company he himself had created. In spite of his crimes, Constantius lauded him as "a prelate above praise," "the wisest of teachers," and "the fittest guide in the Kingdom of Heaven."

The martinet proceeded to harass all church officers, monks, and virgins who would not subscribe to Arian doctrine. He had his henchmen set fire to monasteries, sack private homes, and break into the tombs and mausoleums in search of Athanasius.

One Sunday evening, he sent an army of three thousand to surround a certain cemetery where many of the faithful, hounded from their churches, were engaging in worship. The soldiers laid hold of men, women, and young people, scourging them so brutally that not a few perished.

George denied the privilege of funeral services for the dead. He had a large group of survivors led into exile in chains, not a few showing scars, wounds, and other proofs of torture inflicted by the soldiers.

Word reached Athanasius, who was hiding out in a suburb of Alexandria, of the barbarities put upon the persecuted believers. He considered the idea of appealing to Constantius for clemency for the survivors. But then he learned that the emperor was currently branding him "a cheat and an imposter," "a runaway criminal," and "a wretch who fully deserved death." He surrendered all hopes of a reprieve.

Athanasius left the suburb and retired to the desert, traveling by night. The desert was to be his home for the next six years. He became an itinerant shepherd, ministering to flocks of friendly monks. These simple folk were both proud and delighted to have such a celebrity company with them.

He sojourned with the hermits in Lower Egypt, met with cenobites inhabiting the Nitrian Mountains, and visited monasteries in Upper Egypt and in the pathless solitudes of the Thebais Hills. Often he endured scorching heat by day and numbing cold by night. Periodically, government agents tried to track him down in order to secure his arrest. Wilderness monks then shuttled him from monastery to monastery, from cave to cave, loving him, glorifying in the indomitable and unconquerable spirit of one they called "their invisible patriarch."

On one occasion he was sailing down the Nile on a riverboat. Two assassins, hired by the Arians to kill him, disguised themselves and boarded the vessel. A friendly member of the crew got wind of the plot and warned Athanasius of the danger. He, in turn, double-crossed the assassins by disguising himself and, at the next stop, left the boat under the umbrella of night and once more foiled the scheme of his oppressors.

Again, with government agents closing in on him, a compassionate monk concealed him in a dry desert well where for weeks he was kept safe and alive by the good Samaritan.

In the tempestuous career of Athanasius, the nearest thing to romantic involvement took place during this exile. From time to time he would risk secret excursions back to Alexandria to confer with friends. He always traveled incognito. On one of these nocturnal junkets, a false friend informed Constantius's secret service men of the archbishop's presence. A beautiful virgin, Eudaemonis, sheltered him in her home for several days. The search for the alleged outlaw proved unsuccessful. The agents, frustrated, finally gave up the search. Once more Athanasius had made good his escape.

Unfortunately for Eudaemonis, news of the concealment leaked. George, given the information, arrested the virgin and had her imprisoned and tortured until she all but lost her mind before being released.

As expected, the Arians used the episode as an excuse to heap all kinds of lying slurs on a man whose moral life was blameless. For this tirade Athanasius cared not a snap of his fingers. But when advised of the sufferings of Eudaemonis, he was inconsolable. For nights and days he shed scalding tears. He determined to put a stop to all clandestine meetings in Alexandria.

Chapter 19

Early in the year 363 Constantius died. Julian, nephew of Constantine assumed the purple. He was to rule a mere sixteen months. In character, he represented a curious blend of cleverness and fanaticism. Shortly before taking over his new authority, he publicly repudiated what elements of formal Christianity he had embraced and loudly announced his conversion to paganism. For this reason he was from then on known as Julian the Apostate.

His friend Ammianus Marcellinus has passed on a description of the man:

> *His eyes were fine and flashing, an indication of the nimbleness of his mind. He had handsome eyebrows, a straight nose, a rather large mouth with a drooping lower lip. His neck was thick and slightly bent, his shoulders broad and big. From top to toe he was well-knit, and so was strong and a good runner.*

No sooner had Julian become emperor than he removed the cross and monogram of Christ from the Roman coins and standards and replaced them with heathen symbols. Every morning and every evening he offered sacrifices to the rising and setting sun. He proceeded to surround himself with pagan mystics, sophists, jugglers, soothsayers, babblers, and scoffers. Although he himself never indulged in intoxicating liquors, to taunt the Christian community, he installed pictures of Bacchus, the god of wine, in the basilicas at Emesa and Wpiphaneia. He also renewed and refurbished the neglected heathen shrines and temples with expensive embellishments.

Julian's lifestyle was puzzling. He practiced asceticism; probably, as he did most things, for effect. He let his hair grow long; wore a rough, uncombed beard; loved to display ink-stained hands; and slept on the floor. He prided himself on being a vegetarian. He spurned the simplest laws of sanitation and was without doubt the complete prototype of the modern hippy.

His contemporaries sometimes referred to him as "the ape of Christianity." While renewing and reactivating anti-Christian religions, he sought at the same time to plant the flag of Christian ethics in the quicksand of heathen pantheism. He patterned the priesthood of polytheism after the Christian clergy. Priests had to be constant in their service in the temples and shrines of the gods, live in strict chastity, give alms to the poor, abstain from impure literature, preach sermons based on mythology, and offer prayers to various deities.

Julian himself was fascinated with necromancy, divination, black magic. He studiously pored over the entrails of animals. He learned and applied the types of soothsaying advocated by the Neoplatonists.

For all his freakishness, Julian was surprisingly shrewd. Early in his political career he came to the conclusion that physical persecution of Christians solved nothing. He saw the truth in the famous aphorism of Tertullian, the Carthagian theologian: "The blood of martyrs is seed."

Julian resolved to refrain from violence. The first three centuries of brute force against the church had proven a futile effort to stamp out the faith of the martyrs. He was aware of this. He would, therefore, practice toleration. Everyone was allowed to worship as he pleased. Banished clergymen were permitted to return home.

It was all splendid theory. Just how consistent Julian was is evidenced by the fact that at Edessa, he confiscated all church property and distributed the money among his soldiers. He justified the act, he explained sardonically, because he was in this way helping Christian people to enter the Kingdom of Heaven. Had not their Master taught His followers that riches would exclude them from that blissful sphere? Therefore he was doing them a favor, he claimed.

Julian also promulgated a law that placed state schools under the supervision of heathen instructors. He prohibited instruction in sciences and art, hoping thus to have the Christian youth of the empire grow up in ignorance.

Actually, the emperor had nothing but contempt for the Catholic religion, his vaunted attitude of tolerance notwithstanding. He loathed the movement in its genuine as well as in its counterfeit patterns. His method of destroying the ones he called "godless Galileans," whether orthodox, Arian, or Semi-Arian, was to employ the weapon of sarcastic mockery.

To a degree, Julian was successful in the carrying out of his designs. Church members who had borne the reproach of Christ and been willing to suffer bodily harm defected under the lash of scornful derision, as the Apostate had anticipated. Well has perceptive Gilbert Chesterton suggested to his readers that some who acknowledge the Son of God and would willingly give their bodies to be burned cannot endure the hollow ridicule of the skeptic, and so turn back.

On February 22, 363, Athanasius, taking advantage of Julian's recalling of exiles, journeyed back to Alexandria.

He lost no time summoning delegates to a council. His objectives were threefold: (1) to have the bishops confirm his reinstatement to office; (2) to bring together dissident parties in a fragmented church in loving union; and (3) to clarify certain Christological questions. He succeeded in having the council process all three items. The actions meant restoration of health to a sick church.

One result of the conference was outstanding: the leadership of the organized African diocese had shifted from the shoulders of a power-crazed emperor to the shoulders of Athanasius.

Fully conscious of the transition, Julian broke into a spasm of fury. He openly assailed his enemy as "a meddler," "a foe of the gods," and "a paltry mannikin." He trumpeted, "It has never been my intention that the miscreant should go back to Alexandria as a primate. I now issue a decree that he must quit the city at once."

Julian sent the edict to Alexandrian Christians by the medium of Pythiodorus, a pagan philosopher and magistrate living in Alexandria. Pythiodorus, who hated Athanasius with perfect hatred, delivered the message with undisguised jubilation.

When the Christians received the information, they surrounded Athanasius and wept. This crushing treatment, they wailed, was so unwarranted, so undeserved.

Athanasius comforted the mourners with the thought, "Take heart, my beloved. This is but a passing cloud, and the darkness will soon be gone;" with these haunting words, he began his fourth exile.

Chapter 20

Ironically, Julian's passion for soothsaying became the springboard that led to his undoing.

Infected by the virus of ambition, he elected to break the terms of armistice his father had worked out with Sapor, king of Persia, at the termination of the war. He, the mighty Julian, he told himself, was the man who would be king over the whole civilized world. To fulfill that goal, he would first overrun the Persian army before it could be brought to full strength by Sapor. After that, he would take over nation after nation until there would be no more worlds to conquer. But, he decided, he must be sure of his ground. He would consult the gods on the outcome of his plan.

He sent envoys to the oracles at Delphi, Delos, and Dona to check with the omniscient prophets of the gods. The messengers came back to him all bearing the same advice, "Go and conquer."

The prophet at Delphi was more specific. He promised, "We, all the gods, have marched forth to win trophies of victory at the Wildbeast River; and I, the impetuous battle-stormer Mars, will be the leader."

Julian interpreted the Wildbeast River to mean the Tigris. With childlike confidence in the revelation, he marshalled his legions and personally led them into battle.

The two armies clashed on the east bank of the Tigris River. The Romans decisively won the opening round. Flushed with their success, they pushed the Persians back to the city of Ctesiphon, where the defenders rallied and fought back ferociously. They managed to turn the flow of conflict and force Julian's troops back to the Tigris.

Before Julian's generals could regroup their scattered cadres and counterattack, someone came upon the lifeless form of Julian, his head immersed in the waters of the Tigris, his body stretched out on the shore. No marks of violence were to be seen. Not a person had been there when death had taken over. Most of the Roman soldiers theorized that their leader had taken his life. Whatever the cause of Julian's death, the soldiers of both armies ceased fighting and quietly returned to their respective homes.

During the sixteen months of his fourth exile, Athanasius passed a portion of the time in interior Egypt. At Thebes, the No-Ammon of the Old Testament, he could not but marvel at the sight of the jeweled gates as well as the magnitude of the city, in size the equivalent of Rome. Thebes was checkered with magnificent temples, sphinxes, royal sepulchres, and monuments honoring the dead kings.

Entering Hermopolis and beholding the metropolis wholly given over to idolatry, Athanasius's spirit was stirred within him, as was the Apostle Paul's when he entered Athens. And following Paul's example, in the marketplace he seized every opportunity to talk with any and all willing to engage in a discussion on the subject of religion. To such, as did Paul, he proclaimed "Jesus and the resurrection."

By striking coincidence, the results of Athanasius's evangelistic outreach corresponded to Paul's: some hearers mocked; others said, "We will hear you again;" but certain believed his words. These begged him for further instruction.

In view of the reception, he prolonged his stay in the city several weeks, confirming the new converts in their faith. When he was about to leave, he promised to send them a bishop from Alexandria as soon as the way cleared for him to return home.

From Hermopolis he walked to Karnac, then to Luxor. At Luxor, he drifted awestruck through the stately courts and massive temples, many of them constructed under the direction of Amenophis III, and later embellished by the celebrated Tutankamen — "King Tut."

Leaving Luxor, Athanasius climbed Mt. Libyan. He stood at the summit contemplating the vast plain that rolled away to the west, boundless and bare. He turned and surveyed historic Luxor and Karnac.

I wonder, he reflected, if the Prophet Jeremiah, deported to Egypt, touched these communities, bringing the knowledge of the living and true God over against Egyptian deities, which, having eyes see not, ears and hear not, noses and smell not, hands and feel not, feet and walk not. Possibly I shall be able to come back someday to take up where Jeremiah left off. I pray to God it may be so.

Chapter 21

On June 27, 365, Jovian, chief of the Imperial Guard, inherited Julian's post. Oddly, he attained the honor by the election of his army.

One of the first moves he made was to direct a relative of Julian to convey Julian's remains to Tarsus, the city where Paul was born. Strange paradox: Julian, the man whose life was passionately dedicated to the subversion of the Christian religion, was to be buried near the birthplace of Paul, the man whose life was passionately dedicated to the gospel's triumphal advance.

In appearance, Jovian was so tall that it required a tailor to sew a purple robe large enough to accommodate him. Strikingly handsome, with fair hair and sparkling blue eyes, the new emperor was the object of the adoration of every maiden living in Constantinople. He was known to be jovial, bluff, and sometimes blunt but completely unaffected. He could be labeled a kind of New Testament Nathanael, a character in whom there was no deceit.

From Jovian's youth, he was a zealous crusader for the doctrines espoused by Athanasius. Immediately after attending to the disposal of the body of Julian, he sent this communication to Athanasius:

> *Our royal authority recalls you and wills you to return for the teachings of salvation. Come back, therefore, to the holy church and feed the people of God, and send forth from your heart prayers to God for clemency. For we know through your supplication that we, and all with us who are Christians, shall receive powerful assistance from Almighty God.*

With the letter, Jovian requested a copy of the Nicene Creed for his further study. Athanasius obliged, and with the copy, he included a letter saying:

> *It well becomes a prince dear to God to have instruction, and to desire heavenly things. Thus will my leader truly*

have his heart in the hand of God. We who hold forth the faith of the Catholic Church, give thanks to the Lord for you and we have resolved, after deliberation, to remind you of the faith professed by the Fathers of Nicea.

The relation between Jovian and Athanasius was as beautiful as it was brief — brief because the new emperor wore purple for a period of only a few months.

Jovian quickly showed himself to officiate as an alert and able reformer. He ordered his soldiers to restore the Christian monogram on their banners and shields. He gave back to the churches the franchises and communities commandeered by Julian the Apostate. He recalled from exile the clergymen his predecessor and Constantius had sent to distant places. He also reinstated the bishops Julian had ejected from their sees because of their adherence to the Nicene Creed. He ordered heathen temples dismantled and locked up.

The continuing and insidious diatribe against Athanasius lodged by the Arian syndrome filled Jovian with righteous wrath. He ably answered the charges hurled against his friend:

I know well why Athanasius was accused and banished. I have inquired diligently into the whole affair, and am convinced that he teaches the true faith, and whoever wishes to know what the faith is, let him go and learn it from him. You say he calls you heretics: yes, and it is his duty to do so. It is the duty of all who teach the truth to denounce heresy.

Later, Jovian's anger reached the boiling point. A puppet of the Arians, Lucius, arrived in Alexandria by ship for the purpose of inciting the public against Athanasius. Learning of the campaign, Jovian exclaimed, "Lucius, may the Lord of the universe and the sun and the moon wreak His displeasure on those who sailed with you for not throwing you overboard. And may the ship on which you sailed never again have prosperous winds, and never come safely to port."

In the winter of 364, Jovian, en route from Antioch to Constantinople, stopped in an inn in the city of Dadastana to spend the night. The weather was bitterly cold. The bedroom where he slept proved damp and poorly heated. He never survived the night. The cause of his death was carbon-monoxide poisoning. So passed from earth one of the greatest of rulers. In the gallery of emperors, Jovian stands out as the noblest Roman of them all.

The custom of choosing the emperor by the vote of Roman soldiers continued. On the death of Jovian, the army selected a high officer, Flavius Valentinianus, to succeed him. The election was made at Nicea.

For some peculiar reason, possibly because the voters may have thought Valentinianus needed moral support, they decided that a co-emperor be named. The choice fell on Valentinianus's younger brother, Valens, a private in the ranks. Valentinianus was to rule in the West, Valens in the East. It meant that Egypt, and thus the bishopric of Athanasius, would fall in the sphere of Valens.

Valens turned out to be a kind of nonperson, said to be "made without vigor and feeble without mildness." He was, in fact, more a jellyfish than a man. He went through life agreeing with everyone on every conceivable subject. If there was an iota of conviction in his bones, no one ever discovered it.

Valens quickly showed himself to be an implacable foe of orthodoxy. He was outright venomous in his attitude toward Athanasius. So was his wife, a Jezebel in her own right, who proved to be as domineering over her husband as was Queen Jezebel over Ahab. She was a devoted Arian.

Incited by her constant nagging, Valens resumed persecutions against the Christians. Soon after his taking on the emperorship, he adjourned a council assembled at Lampsacus. The reason: he received word that the bishops were preparing to condemn Arianism.

Valens took up his residence in Nicodemia. When a delegation of bishops holding Athanasian convictions called on him to present a plan for clemency, he ordered them arrested. Unwilling to execute the visitors in public lest he be branded a murderer, he commanded his soldiers to place the eighty on board a ship. The ship was to be put out to sea and set on fire. This was done. The sailors escaped in a lifeboat. Every one of the prisoners perished in flames.

Valens knew practically nothing about theology. He appointed as his counselor on religious matters an archenemy of Athanasius named Euxidius. This perfidious fanatic, who could not stand the sight of Athanasius, plagued Valens without let-up until he agreed to the banishment of the archbishop.

On October 5, 367, a company of soldiers, carrying out the edict, broke into the Church of Saint Dionysius, where Athanasius was living. Athanasius left the church and hid in a tomb in the churchyard. When he found out from a loyal friend that the time was favorable, he left the tomb, escaped from Alexandria, and took refuge in the home of a friend living on a bank of the New River.

It was the fifth and final time the harried primate was to be driven from his parish.

Chapter 22

With the approach of his final years in the service of the church —
he was sixty six — Athanasius had in principle identified himself
with the company of pilgrims mentioned in the book of Hebrews:
"They wandered about in deserts, and in mountains, and in dens
and caves of the earth." So inured was he to adversity that he had
learned to accept suffering, not in a masochistic sense, but rather
in the spirit exercised by Paul. He could and often did in complete
honesty quote the great Apostle: "For Christ's sake, I delight in
infirmities, in insults, in hardships, in persecutions and distresses."
The cloud which he once predicted would soon pass was somewhat
delayed in evaporating.

Early one evening while drifting down the Nile River in a
riverboat near Hermopolis, suddenly his attention was called to a
group of bishops and monks gathered on the bank of the stream.
They were carrying lanterns and torches. One of the bishops shouted
his name. He recognized the voice as belonging to his friend, Abbot
Theodore.

"Yes, Theodore," he called out.

"I am here with some of your comrades," Theodore responded.
"Please come ashore."

Athanasius requested the steersman of the boat to deliver him
to the shore. The steersman obliged.

A company of the archbishop's followers were there with a
donkey. They formed a procession and escorted Athanasius into
Hermopolis, all the while chanting portions of the Psalms. In little
time, word buzzed about the city that Archbishop Athanasius was
present. Crowds quickly materialized as the procession wove
through the streets to the cheering of hundreds of loyal admirers.

The reception so moved Athanasius that he turned to Theodore
and said, "It is not we who are the heroes, my friend. It is those
who are devoted to humility and obedience. Blessed indeed, and
worthy of all praise, are the ones who carry the cross."

Before they settled down for the night in the home of a Christian
friend, Theodore said to Athanasius, "I must warn you that Valens
has made it known that he has set a price on your head. It is the

reason we interrupted your river trip. Downstream, guards have been waiting to arrest you and take you to him."

The incident occurred on a Saturday. Theodore urged Athanasius to remain in Hermopolis over the Sunday. The abbot urged him to deliver a sermon in the local church the next day. Athanasius gladly yielded. But after the service, he admitted that the current pressures were putting him under an almost unendurable strain.

Just then, a resident of Hermopolis came bursting into the church and panted, "Quick! Valens's men are coming here from the south to arrest you. Come, we have a boat at the dock ready to take you north."

Theodore and another abbot helped Athanasius hurry to the Nile. There, a riverboat awaited them. Since at that point the Nile flowed southward, four monks were required to turn the skiff north against the current. The two abbots made Athanasius comfortable in the stern and then seated themselves near him.

While the monks on the shore strained at their task, Athanasius, with closed eyes, poured out his soul in almost violent prayer. The recent attempts on his life, as he had confessed to Theodore, were bringing him to the verge of a breakdown. As was his custom, he sought relief in the presence of God.

He ended his prayer. In the glow of the clear, velvety evening, the abbots caught his wan smile. He said, "I am often more calm in persecution than when I am at rest. There is invariably, however, an aftermath that enfeebles me. Still if God wills and I am to be slain . . ."

At the mention of the word *slain*, the abbots exchanged glances. Athanasius observed the meeting in their eyes and said, "Is it because you think I fear death? No . . ."

Theodore held up a hand. "My dear friend," he said quietly, "our God knows what is best for His children. While you were praying, a brother called to us from the shore and said, 'Valens is dead.' "

Athanasius received the news stoically. The abbots saw him bow his head. His lips moved in silent prayer.

Chapter 23

Athanasius lived out the remaining span of his life in comparative tranquility. Joyfully he devoted his gifts to preaching, counseling, and writing books and essays. He also busied himself in lengthy correspondence, giving out advice and encouragement to his younger fellow ministers and priests bothered with questions of doctrine, polity, and church discipline. To the end of his life, he continued to defend the pronouncements of the Council of Nicea.

In an encyclical letter he wrote:

Let the Confession of Faith, drawn up by the fathers at Nicea, stand good; for it is correct, and capable of overthrowing any impious heresy, and especially the Arian error which insults the Word of God, and necessarily falls into impiety against the Holy Spirit.

In the autumn of 373, he convened his last council. This body unanimously certified the actions of the Council of Rome, which in turn had moved to enforce the authority of the Nicene Creed; it also decided to excommunicate the obstreperous Arian bishop, Uracius. The council, too, sent out a synodical letter emphasizing the need to remain faithful to Christ, the Lord of the church, and to His truths.

Close friends of Athanasius observed an arresting feature of his final years of office. They detected in his writings and oral contacts overtones of flexibility — a bending, a mellowness formerly missing. They remembered that there had been times when in controversy the callow archdeacon had in anger branded his enemies as "chameleons," "hydras," "eels," "cuttlefrogs," "gnats," "beetles," "leeches," even "athe-ists." In these last years, Athanasius no longer used these severe epithets. In the venerable archbishop, people noted that impatience had given way to patience, hardness to tenderness, intemperance to moderation, bitterness to sweetness.

The point was illustrated in one of his latest books, *Against Apollinarianism*: in it he wrote against a teaching that denied the integral humanity of Jesus. He corrected the errors of the cult but out of consideration for the merits of the originator never so much as mentioned his name.

A second example occurred when an African candidate for the office of bishop, a young man named Siderius, received the laying on of hands in an unconstitutional manner. The Council of Nicea had prescribed that at least three bishops should officially set aside the candidates for ordination. In the case of Siderius, a single bishop conducted the ceremony; it was clear breach of rule. When the mistake was pointed out to Athanasius, whose duty it was to approve or disapprove the ordination, instead of "going by the book," the archbishop generously approved what had taken place.

One of the excellent contacts developed in the sunset of his life was his relation with Basil of Caesarea. This promising youth had received his education in philosophy, rhetoric, and mathematics at Athens. On completing his studies, Basil took up the monastic life. From his father he had inherited a huge fortune. Unlike the rich young ruler of New Testament note, he distributed all his goods to feed the poor. He would gladly have spent his life in isolation; he loved the mountains and forests. "Silent solitude," he was heard to say, "is the beginning of the purification of the soul."

He became known as a marvelous wordsmith. He had the soul of a poet. For sheer literary prowess, there was no peer in the pantheon of the early church fathers. Referring to the grandeur of nature, he wrote:

> *The river of my wilderness, more rapid than any other I know, breaks upon the wall of projecting rock, and rolls foaming into the abyss; to the mountain traveler, a charming, wonderful sight; to the natives, profitable for its abundant fisheries. Shall I describe to you the fertilizing vapors which rise from the [moistened] earth, the cool air which rises from the [moving] mirror of the waters? Shall I tell you of the lovely singing of the birds and the richness of the blooming plants? What delights me is the silence of the place.*

In 364, the church had forced him to come out of isolation and made him, against his wishes, a presbyter, or elder. Six years later, the church consecrated him archbishop of Cappadocian Caesarea.

Despite his exposure to pagan philosophy, Basil early learned to know and love and proclaim the teachings of Athanasius. He cultivated a tremendous admiration for the archbishop as well. Although the two never met, they carried on a stimulating and edifying correspondence. Basil often referred to the Alexandrian as "my spiritual father." On one occasion, when some churchmen attacked Basil because they decided his view of the Holy Spirit was "hazy," Athanasius stoutly defended "my son in the faith."

The older man felt that as the time of his passing was at hand, he might find consolation in the hope that his mantle would rest fittingly on the shoulders of Basil — that the archbishop of Caesarea, though handicapped by poor health, would nevertheless assume his post. Blessedly, Athanasius lived to learn that mantle was where he desired. Filled with joy, he breathed the prayer of Simeon in the temple of Jerusalem, "Now Lord, let Thy servant depart in peace."

His memory was still green, his mind and conscience clear, as he prepared to pass over the great divide. He called to remembrance his services for Christ and the church; his own victories and defeats; his ecstatic joys and deep depressions; his brushes with emperors and with beggars; his plans, often ending in disappointment and frustration; and his bright hopes gloriously fulfilled. This was his heritage.

His exodus from earth was as unspectacular as his career had been dramatic. After eighty years of robust activity, his hair was as white as a fleecy cloud, his tired frame frail and worn. But his spirit was as fresh and buoyant as it had been in adolescence. On a gentle spring evening, he whispered his final prayer, serenely lay down with death, and fell asleep in Jesus.

A final tribute came from the pen of Gregory of Naziazon: "He ended his life in a holy old age and went to keep company with his fathers, the patriarchs, prophets, apostles, and martyrs who had fought valiantly for the truth — as he had."

3rd Printing

Augustine, The Farmer's Boy of Tagaste
by P. De Zeeuw

C. MacDonald in *The Banner of Truth*: Augustine was one of the great teachers of the Christian Church, defending it against many heretics. This interesting publication should stimulate and motivate all readers to extend their knowledge of Augustine and his works.

J. Sawyer in *Trowel & Sword*: . . . It is informative, accurate historically and theologically, and very readable. My daughter loved it (and I enjoyed it myself). An excellent choice for home and church libraries.

Time: A.D. 354-430   Age: 9-99
ISBN 0-921100-05-1   Can.$7.95 U.S.$6.90

4th Printing

William of Orange-The Silent Prince
by W.G. Van de Hulst

Byron Snapp in *The Counsel of Chalcedon*: Here is a Christian who persevered in the Christian faith when the cause seemed lost and he was being pursued by government authorities. Impoverished, he was offered great wealth to deny his principles. He refused. He remembered that true wealth is found in obeying God. . . . Although written for children, this book can be greatly enjoyed by adults. No doubt Christians of all ages will be encouraged by the life of William of Orange . . . This book is a great choice for families to read and discuss together.

Time: 1533-1584   Age: 7-99
ISBN 0-921100-15-9   Can.$11.95 U.S.$9.90

Quintus by R. Weerstand
A Story About the
Persecution of Christians
at the Time of Emperor Nero

The history of the Church in A.D. 64 is written with blood and tears. This book, based on historical facts, relates what happened in Rome in the summer of that year. It is a gripping chronicle. In the story we meet Quintus, the central character. He is a typical Roman boy, who through a number of ordeals experiences the grace of God.

Time: A.D. 64   Age: 12-99
ISBN 1-894666-70-4   Can.$9.95 U.S.$8.90

Hubert Ellerdale by W. Oak Rhind
A Tale of the Days of Wycliffe

Christine Farenhorst in *Christian Renewal*: Christians often tend to look on the Reformation as the pivotal turning point in history during which the Protestants took off the chains of Rome. This small work of fiction draws back the curtains of history a bit further than Luther's theses. Wycliffe was the morning star of the Reformation and his band of Lollards a band of faithful men who were persecuted because they spoke out against salvation by works. Hubert Ellerdale was such a man and his life (youth, marriage, and death), albeit fiction, is set parallel to Wycliffe's and Purvey's.

Rhind writes with pathos and the reader can readily identify with his lead characters. This novel deserves a well-dusted place in a home, school, or church library.

Time: 1380-1420	**Age: 13-99**
ISBN 0-921100-09-4	**Can.$12.95 U.S.$10.90**

A Theatre in Dachau by Hermanus Knoop

Rev. Jerome Julien in *The Outlook*, Those dreadful years of Nazi oppression in the Netherlands are catalogued here in an amazing way. Not only Jews, but faithful ministers of God's Word were touched, too. And from the caldron of torture the Lord received some of His servants to Himself: Revs. Kapteyn, Sietsma, and Tunderman. Others came through it, refined in God's crucible . . . The beauty of this book is found in the constant Christian testimony found in it. It is more than an account of atrocity; it is his personal reactions as a firmly founded believer to whom the Holy Spirit continued to apply God's marvellous Word. Every believer should read this little volume. This reviewer could hardly put it down because it is so moving.

Time: 1940-1943	**Age: 14-99**
ISBN 0-921100-20-5	**Can.$14.95 U.S.$12.90**

Israel's Hope and Expectation
by Rudolf Van Reest

G. Nederveen in *Clarion*: This is one of the best novels I have read of late. I found it captivating and hard to put down. Here is a book that is not time-bound and therefore it will never be outdated.

The story takes place around the time of Jesus' birth. It is written by someone who has done his research about the times between the Old and New Testament period. The author informs you in an easy style about the period of the Maccabees . . . Van Reest is a good storyteller. His love for the Bible and biblical times is evident from the start. He shows a good knowledge of the customs and mannerisms in Israel. Many fine details add to the quality of the book. You will be enriched in your understanding of the ways in the Old Testament.

Time: Inter-Testament Period	**Age: 15-99**
ISBN 0-921100-22-1	**Can.$19.95 U.S.$17.90**

Salt in His Blood
The Life of Michael De Ruyter
by William R. Rang

Liz Buist in *Reformed Perspective*: This book is a fictional account of the life of Michael de Ruyter, who as a schoolboy already preferred life at sea to being at school . . . This book is highly recommended as a novel way to acquiring knowledge of a segment of Dutch history, for avid young readers and adults alike.

Time: 1607-1676   **Age: 10-99**
ISBN 0-921100-59-0   **Can.$10.95 U.S.$9.90**

The Romance of Protestantism
by Deborah Alcock

The Romance of Protestantism addresses one of the most damaging and (historically) effective slanders against the Reformed faith, which is that it is cold and doctrinaire. What a delight to find a book which documents the true warmth of the Protestant soul. I recommend this book highly.
— Douglas Wilson, editor of *Credenda/Agenda*

Time: 1300-1700   **Age: 12-99**
ISBN 0-921100-88-4   **Can.$ 11.95 U.S.$ 9.90**

Love in Times of Reformation
by William P. Balkenende

N.N. in *The Trumpet*: This historical novel plays in The Netherlands during the rise of the protestant Churches, under the persecution of Spain, in the latter half of the sixteenth century. Breaking with the Roman Catholic Church in favor of the new faith is for many an intense struggle. Anthony Tharret, the baker's apprentice, faces his choice before the R.C. Church's influenced Baker's Guild. His love for Jeanne la Solitude, the French Huguenot refugee, gives a fresh dimension to the story. Recommended! Especially for young people.

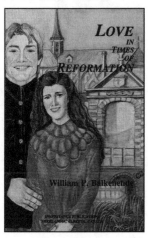

Time: 1560-1585   **Age: 14-99**
ISBN 0-921100-32-9   **Can.$8.95 U.S.$7.90**

The Governor of England
by Marjorie Bowen
A Novel on Oliver Cromwell

An historical novel in which the whole story of Cromwell's dealings with Parliament and the King is played out. It is written with dignity and conviction, and with the author's characteristic power of grasping the essential details needed to supply colour and atmosphere for the reader of the standard histories.

Time: 1645-1660   Age: 14-99
ISBN 0-921100-58-2   Can.$17.95 U.S.$15.90

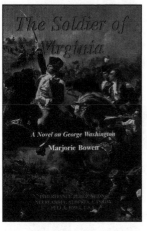

The Soldier of Virginia
A Novel on George
Washington by Marjorie Bowen

Originally published in 1912, this is a fictionalized biography on America's first President by one of the best authors of historical fiction.

Time: 1755-1775   Age: 14-99
ISBN 0-921100-99-X   Can.$14.95 U.S.$12.90

The Seventh Earl by Grace Irwin

A dramatized biography on Anthony Ashley Cooper, the Seventh Earl of Shaftesbury, who is most widely remembered as a 19th-century British philanthropist and factory reformer. "This is Grace Irwin's strongest and most poignant book . . . I have been moved and enriched by my hours with The Seventh Earl," wrote V.R. Mollenkott.

Time: 1801-1885   Age: 14-99
ISBN 0-8028-6059-1   Can.$11.95 U.S.$9.95

A Stranger in a Strange Land
by Leonora Scholte

John E. Marshall in The Banner of Truth: This is a delightful book. It tells the story of H.P. Scholte, a preacher in the Netherlands, who, being persecuted for his faith in his own country, emigrated to the U.S.A., and there established a settlement in Pella, Iowa, in the midst of the vast undeveloped prairie . . . It is a most heartwarming and instructive story.

Time: 1825-1880   Age: 14-99
ISBN 0-921100-01-9   Can.$7.95 U.S.$6.90

Coronation of Glory
by Deborah Meroff

The true story of seventeen-year-old Lady Jane Grey, Queen of England for nine days.

"Miss Meroff . . . has fictionalized the story of Lady Jane Grey in a thoroughly absorbing manner . . . she has succeeded in making me believe this is what really happened. I kept wanting to read on — the book is full of action and interest."
— Elisabeth Elliot

Time: 1537-1554   **Age: 14-99**
ISBN 0-921100-78-7   Can.$14.95 U.S.$12.90

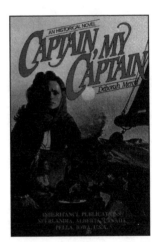

Captain My Captain by **Deborah Meroff**

Willy-Jane VanDyken in *The Trumpet*: This romantic novel is so filled with excitement and drama, it is difficult to put it down once one has begun it. Its pages reflect the struggle between choosing Satan's ways or God's ways. Mary's struggles with materialism, being a submissive wife, coping with the criticism of others, learning how to deal with sickness and death of loved ones, trusting in God and overcoming the fear of death forces the reader to reflect on his own struggles in life. This story of Mary Ann Patten (remembered for being the first woman to take full command of a merchant sailing ship) is one that any teen or adult reader will enjoy. It will perhaps cause you to shed a few tears but it is bound to touch your heart and encourage you in your faith.

Time: 1837-1861   **Age: 14-99**
ISBN 0-921100-79-5   Can.$14.95 U.S.$12.90

Journey Through the Night
by Anne De Vries

After the second world war, Anne De Vries, one of the most popular novelists in The Netherlands, was commissioned to capture in literary form the spirit and agony of those five harrowing years of Nazi occupation. The result was Journey Through the Night, a four volume bestseller that has gone through more than thirty printings in The Netherlands.

"An Old Testament Professor of mine who bought the books could not put them down — nor could I."   — Dr. Edwin H. Palmer

Time: 1940-1945   **Age: 10-99**
ISBN 0-921100-25-6   Can.$19.95 U.S.$16.90

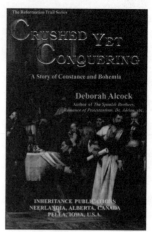

Crushed Yet Conquering
by Deborah Alcock

A gripping story filled with accurate historical facts about John Huss and the Hussite wars. **Hardly any historical novel can be more captivating and edifying than this book.** Even if Deborah Alcock was not the greatest of nineteenth century authors, certainly she is our most favourite.

— Roelof & Theresa Janssen

Time: 1414-1436   **Age: 11-99**
ISBN 1-894666-01-1   **Can.$19.95 U.S.$16.90**

The Spanish Brothers by Deborah Alcock

Christine Farenhorst in *Christian Renewal*: This historical novel, which is set in Spain a number of years after the Reformation, deals with the discovery of Reformed truth in that country . . . Two brothers, one a soldier and the other a student of theology, are the protagonists. Sons of a nobleman who disappeared when they were children, their search for him leads both to a confrontation with the Gospel. How they react, how their friends and relatives react to them, and what their struggles and thoughts are, form the main body of the book.

An excellent read, this book should be in every church and home library.

Time: 1550-1565   **Age: 14-99**
ISBN1-894666-02-x   **Can.$14.95 U.S.$12.90**

By Far Euphrates by Deborah Alcock
A Tale on Armenia in the 19th century

Alcock has provided sufficient graphics describing the atrocities committed against the Armenian Christians to make the reader emotionally moved by the intense suffering these Christians endured at the hands of Muslim Turks and Kurds. At the same time, the author herself has confessed to not wanting to provide full detail, which would take away from the focus on how those facing death did so with peace, being confident they would go to see their LORD, and so enjoy eternal peace. **As such it is not only an enjoyable novel, but also encouraging reading.** These Christians were determined to remain faithful to their God, regardless of the consequences.

Time: 1887-1895   **Age: 11-99**
ISBN 1-894666-00-3   **Can.$14.95 U.S.$12.90**